I0818411

75
150
145
140
125
95
34

THE ART OF
ANTIQUING
IN FRANCE

Text by Sharon Santoni
With the assistance of Madeleine Piggott

Photography by

Johanna Biscarrat: p. 145

Joanna Chomu: pp. 74, 90–91

Camille Cuvelier: pp. 135 (l), 136 (l)

Galerie Quattro: p. 68

Jacky Hobbs: pp. 190 (r), 191, 193 (r), 194 (r), 195 (r), 211

Joanna Maclennan: front cover inset, pp. 1, 3, 13, 15, 24 (l), 25 (r), 30, 37, 40, 42–44, 47, 50–51, 57, 60, 63–65, 71, 77, 109, 112, 114–129, 158 (r), 161, 180, 182, 190 (l), 196 (r), 197, 208, 236, 238–240

Sharon Santoni: front cover background, endpapers, pp. 2, 4, 10, 12 (l), 16, 19, 24 (r), 25 (l), 27, 28, 31, 41, 49, 52, 55, 58, 59, 66–67, 70, 75, 78, 82, 83, 92, 96 (r), 98, 100, 101 (l), 102–105, 110, 111, 131, 134 (l), 135 (r), 136 (r), 137, 138, 140, 146–149, 152 (r), 157, 159, 171, 174 (r), 175, 178, 183, 194 (l), 195 (l), 198, 199, 202–207, 212, 215, 219, 237

Franck Schmitt: pp. 8, 12 (r), 14, 20–23, 32–35, 38, 48, 56, 62, 72, 73, 81, 85–89, 95, 96 (l), 97, 101 (r), 106–107, 113, 133, 134 (r), 141, 142, 151, 152 (l), 153, 154, 158 (l), 160, 162–170, 172, 174 (l), 176, 177, 181, 184–188, 192, 193 (l), 196 (l), 201, 222–223, 226–228

Artists' Credits

p. 32: © Renée Carpentier-Wintz

p. 33: © Sophie Morisse

pp. 98 and 100 (r): Jean Picart Le Doux © Adagp, Paris, 2026

p. 100 (l): Jean Lurçat © Maison-atelier Lurçat / Adagp, Paris, 2026

PAGES 1–4
Framed ex-votos make a striking display. A pair of century-old wooden doors with their original patina. Eighteenth-century decorated cardboard boxes take pride of place in front of a paper screen. The Village des Brocanteurs in the small town of Lectoure.

PAGE 8
A carefully curated display at the Foire de Chatou.

Editorial director: Kate Mascaro
Editor: Helen Adedotun
Administration manager: Delphine Montagne
Design and typesetting: Claude-Olivier Four
Cover design: Audrey Sednaoui
Copyediting: Lindsay Porter
Proofreading: Penelope Isaac
Indexing: Chris Bell
Production: Elodie Conjat
Color separation: Hyphen, Italy
Printed in Slovenia by Florjancic

© Éditions Flammarion, Paris, 2026
All rights reserved. No part of this publication may be reproduced in any form or by any means, electronic, photocopy, information retrieval system, or otherwise, without written permission from
Éditions Flammarion
82 Rue Saint-Lazare
75009 Paris

editions.flammarion.com
@flammarioninternational

26 27 28 3 2 1

ISBN: 978-2-08-048241-9

Legal Deposit: 03/2026

Flammarion is actively committed to reducing the ecological footprint of its publications. The book you hold in your hands was printed on paper made from wood sourced from sustainably managed forests, using vegetable-based inks, by a printer committed to environmental protection.

SHARON SANTONI

THE ART OF ANTIQUING IN FRANCE

Flea Markets - Brocantes - Antique Shops

Flammarion
PARIS • SINCE 1875

FUCUS
N°6
C
N°8
C

Contents

Introduction

chiner **(verb, French):** the activity of buying antiques and bric-a-brac. A national pastime, the art of antiquing is an integral part of the country's identity and is the reason why every French home boasts an endearing blend of old and new.

Where It All Began

My earliest memory of buying antiques in France occurred decades ago, when my not-yet-husband and I moved into our first apartment in a suburb of Paris. Situated on the edge of the Bois de Vincennes, it was a small, ground-floor apartment with a tiny terrace and tons of charm. It was our first home—unfurnished, and more than a little bare. We bought a bed, and hung all our clothes into the built-in closet, but besides that, we had no other furniture. We were young and in love, and while the barren interior didn't stop us from being happy, it wasn't so practical. Shortly after our move, a large antique fair and *brocante* was announced in a nearby town—the ideal opportunity to furnish the apartment! We set ourselves a budget and drew up our wish list. We were determined to find a table, two chairs, and maybe a sofa, and felt confident in our ability to bring home these necessities. We set off in our old car, and spent a lovely day immersed in color and design, chatting with vendors, and considering the different ways we could spend our hard-earned funds. At the end of the day we returned home triumphant. We had blown our budget but we were thrilled. We pulled our haul out of the car: not a table, nor chairs, nor even a sofa, but a painting!

Today, that painting is still the heart of our home—a beautiful early twentieth-century portrait of two women, standing tall and facing the artist. They may be friends or sisters. Their dress is circa 1930, and their gazes are kind but all-seeing; they are confident and calm. The canvas is unframed, simply stretched over a support, and that is fine. We have moved home many times since that first apartment and the painting has accompanied us from one place to the next. It's said that the true test of a good buy is not the price or the market value of an item, but how long you enjoy it after the purchase. These two ladies came into our lives over thirty years ago, and I have never tired of their company.

FACING PAGE
This postwar portrait of two ladies—my first significant antique purchase—has accompanied my family for decades.

The moral of this story is never to go shopping for antiques with a list. I quickly learned that antiquing is less about checking off items and more about opening your mind and heart to serendipity. You go to an antique market hoping to be touched, to feel a connection, and—ideally—to fall in love. There are still a few missed opportunities that haunt me decades later, but even from those early days there was no doubt about it—I was hooked.

When we left Paris for the Normandy countryside, a new world opened up: *brocantes* and *foires à tout*—informal bric-a-brac markets filled with every item imaginable. I'd never experienced anything like them in my native England, or elsewhere in France. In misty, early morning fields, a mix of vendors would unpack a jumble of paintings, zinc watering cans, linen sheets, tableware, furniture, and so much more. Those were the days when attics and barns still needed emptying—the French term for these rural garage sales of bric-a-brac, *vide-grenier*, translates literally as "empty attic." Old country houses were often passed down through the generations, lying untouched for a hundred years or more, chock full of their original items. When ownership finally changed hands, their contents were dealt with swiftly. Generation's worth of "stuff" would be cleared, and everything—from furniture to tools to linens—was sold as it lay, dusty and covered in cobwebs, simply begging to be loved again. At these weekend fairs, it wasn't unusual to see trucks arriving with box after box of china, glasses, bedding, and flowerpots, as well as chairs and even whole wardrobes, ready to be picked through. A small crowd would gather discreetly and the buying would begin. These shopping sprees became a regular fixture on my calendar. During the week, I would track

ABOVE, LEFT
Pharmacy boxes promoting soaps and ointments.

ABOVE, RIGHT
Late-nineteenth century trinket boxes.

FACING PAGE
Antique dealers have an instinctive flair for design and display, especially at L'Isle-sur-la-Sorgue.

the announcements of nearby fairs and put together a plan of attack. Come Sunday morning, I would creep out of the house while the family was still asleep and drive from one fair to the next, filling up my car as I went. Thanks to my early start, I was able to make it back home just as the family was getting up, bringing them fresh baguettes and croissants along with my *brocante* hauls.

Crucial to my antique-buying experience was a dealer, Laurent, who I met at that time: a gifted man with a sure eye and the ability to turn his hand to any restoration project. He soon became a good family friend, and it was under his guidance that I discovered the world of professional antique buyers. We often hit the Sunday morning fairs together at dawn, and moved through them methodically, rejoicing in each other's finds, meeting up with other dealers, and comparing notes. I couldn't have wished for a better education. He taught me key phrases to use when negotiating, and by observing him among his friends and fellow dealers, I came to understand their world: one of friendly competition, pooled knowledge, and a shared love of discovery.

With time, many dealers also became acquaintances and friends. I got to know their style, and they mine. While one vendor could be counted on for paintings, since we shared the same taste, another would ask me ahead of the next fair if I was interested in a particular set of china, or some beautiful dining chairs. It is a world of trust, where your word is your honor, and reputations are built over several years. Each transaction is part of the learning process and a thread that connects you to an ever-broadening web of relationships.

Mixed in among the professional antique dealers at these country fairs were private vendors, gradually parting with pieces from their own homes—

ABOVE, LEFT
Antique stores often carry a wide and varied selection, from chandeliers to busts to medici vases.

ABOVE, RIGHT
Paintings curated on a theme have a greater impact.

ABOVE, LEFT
Vintage lamps in shades of green with fluted glass.

ABOVE, RIGHT
Barbotine plates by Sarreguemines.

perhaps preparing to move or simply ready for a change. I remember one particular lady with a tiny painting that I loved at first sight. The price was steep, so I made a counteroffer, which she declined. The following year, she returned with a new selection, and that same little painting was tucked among her things. I tried again, and again she said no. It wasn't until the third year, when we crossed paths once more, that she finally smiled and accepted my offer. I gratefully snatched up the painting and took it to a professional framer the very next day. I still love it as much today.

One lesson every antique lover learns—sooner or later—is the price of hesitation. That short pause, the seemingly harmless phrase, "I'll think about it and come back," can haunt you for years. For me, it concerned a table. Twenty years ago, in the dim corner of a newly discovered *brocante* shop, I spotted it: the perfect desk. It was beautifully proportioned, made from warm, soft-toned wood, with elegant carvings that gave it just the right amount of presence. I fell for it immediately, but I was in a rush—late for the school pickup—and told myself I'd return the next morning for a closer look. Foolishly, I didn't ask the dealer to hold it. When I came back the next day, there it was—already wrapped for shipping. It had been sold: "*Elle est vendue, madame*," he said kindly, but firmly. I tried everything. I'm ashamed to admit that I even offered to pay more, but he was an honorable man, and the deal was done.

I've never forgotten that table. And I've never made the same mistake again. When I see something that speaks to me, I act. Because in the world of antiques, the only thing worse than buyer's remorse is missing out on the perfect purchase.

Antiquing Today

Fast forward a decade or two, and the era of the overflowing country fair has quietly faded. Some good fairs remain, but they're rarer now, as top dealers focus on more high-profile venues. Still, the tradition of buying at a *foire à tout* or *vide-grenier* is alive and well. In the countryside, this might unfold in a field, with random wares, some older than others, spilling out of the backs of cars and trucks for inspection by potential buyers. In towns across France, street fairs are often announced in the local paper, online, or on flyers stuck to walls or lampposts. These are places to get sidetracked on your way to the bakery on a Sunday morning, or to take a family walk after a long, lazy lunch. In Paris, the weekend browse might begin at a local event. Pop-up fairs appear throughout the year—especially in summer—scattered across the city's many arrondissements. You could try the regular outdoor stands at Porte de Vanves, or, of course, a full day at the Puces de Saint-Ouen, the famed flea market situated to the north of Paris, where, given enough time, almost anything can be found. Regular buyers tend to have their preferred vendors and go-to addresses. Over time, they come to know the specialties of each stall or shop and head to the appropriate address for their needs. For high-end and particularly beautiful antiques, those in the know may head to the 7th arrondissement to visit the stores along Rue de l'Université and up toward Place Furstemberg in the 6th. There, you'll find the aristocracy of dealers—many of whom keep a second outpost at the Puces de Saint-Ouen—who display their wares with gallery-like restraint.

ABOVE, LEFT
Epoque et Patine are known for their particularly beautiful stands at the Foire de Chatou.

ABOVE, RIGHT
Stone busts against a tapestry backdrop make for a dramatic scene at Stéphane Olivier's Paris boutique.

However your interest begins, there are so many good reasons to choose antiques over modern alternatives. At the very least, it is more environmentally friendly to repurpose than to throw away and replace with new. Beyond sustainability, antiques lend a quiet sense of continuity and character. From a drawer with fine dovetail joints to an irregular, handblown glass, each piece reflects traditional craftsmanship and the materials of its time, which are often finer than those used for new items—compare, for example, an antique cherry side table with a particleboard equivalent from a contemporary retail chain. Antiques prompt us to notice everyday beauty, honor the skill of bygone artisans, and bring the accumulated stories and patina of generations into our homes, adding depth and warmth to the spaces we inhabit.

Whether you're browsing a village *brocante* or stepping into a refined antique gallery, navigating this world becomes even more enjoyable when you immerse yourself in its culture. Building relationships and taking part in rituals are part of the experience, enriching your understanding and deepening your connection to each piece you bring home. This may sound daunting for the occasional visitor to France, but simply getting to know vendors, returning to favorite fairs, and embracing the drama at auctions are surprisingly effective places to start.

Antique Stores Versus *Brocantes*

Understanding the nuance

You'll quickly realize that a *brocante* is not the same as an antique shop. Secondhand dealers fall into two distinct categories: *brocanteurs* and *antiquaires*. While both deal in pre-loved objects, they deliver very different experiences—and offer very different treasures. The beauty of collecting lies in a savvy mix of the two. Antiques lend gravitas and a sense of history; *brocantes* bring warmth and character. A Louis XV armoire sharing space with a vintage bird cage or a pair of mid-century armchairs results in a home that feels layered and alive, shaped by your own eye and instinct. These pieces don't simply coexist, they converse, and together they weave a richly textured narrative of French history, design, and personal style.

Antiquaires

Distinguished by their expertise and discerning eye, *antiquaires*, or antique dealers, specialize in high-value antiques—that is, objects over one hundred years old. They generally operate from well-organized, curated stores with regular hours, or from antique fairs, offering fine furniture, signed artworks, and rare collectibles. With a focus on quality and authenticity, these dealers cater to antiquing connoisseurs and buyers with specialized tastes. Woodwork is highly polished, crystal chandeliers gleam, and silverware is solid. These items are prized not only for their age but for their craftsmanship, rarity, and historical context. Many dealers maintain off-site storage or a second location, allowing them to rotate displays, source rare pieces, and meet bespoke requests. Genuine antique dealers are typically highly knowledgeable, with a deep understanding of art history, materials, and provenance. They work with passion, and often restore pieces themselves, or commission another expert to refurbish an item before putting it up for sale.

Brocanteurs

By contrast, *brocanteurs*—flea market or bric-a-brac vendors—operate in a more relaxed world of secondhand treasures. This is a different way to repurpose old objects, far removed from the displays of highly polished furniture and priceless paintings. *Brocante* dealers are hoarders—their stores are often charmingly haphazard, and their inventories eclectic.

Brocante culture is woven into the fabric of French life. Almost every town or village hosts annual *brocante* fairs, where locals set up stalls filled with possessions that they have inherited, or have been storing for years. These are social events as much as markets, and they offer a glimpse into how the French live with and value the objects of their past. A French *brocante* might yield 1920s enamel coffee pots, worn cutting boards, linen dish towels, mid-century maps, zinc watering cans, ceramics, furniture, and more. These items may be collectible, or simply well loved. A *brocanteur* may also deal in vintage items—typically defined as being at least twenty years old but not yet antique. Vintage pieces reflect the style and spirit of a specific era—like 1950s café chairs or 1980s lighting—and collecting these pieces that feel emblematic of their time is often about nostalgia and design. While they may not meet the formal definition of an antique, they still convey the beauty of age and use.

At the heart of a *brocante* lies the art of repurposing old objects, of giving them new life and function. Many dealers dye faded linens, reimagine wicker trays as wall decorations, turn vintage trunks into side tables, or transform old medicine bottles into bud vases. In this way, they ignite a creative spark in their customers, urging them to see the hidden possibilities of objects that might otherwise have been overlooked or dismissed.

While shopping for items at a *brocante* may come with a lower price tag, this isn't the only allure: it's the thrill of discovering a forgotten object that fits perfectly into a modern home. Seek out unique pieces that speak to your personal style or those with potential for transformation. Amidst the array of choices, just remember William Morris's timeless counsel, from his "The Beauty of Life" lecture (1880): "Have nothing in your house that you do not know to be useful, or believe to be beautiful."

I'm honored to introduce to you, through these pages, the world of French antiques and *brocante* finds that I have come to love so much. I hope that you'll find inspiration and information that will encourage you to explore and discover the many facets of this magnificent culture. You may meet some of my favorite dealers, and you will surely find your own. The key is to enjoy the moment, and never stop learning along the way.

On the last Sunday of each month, Sandrine Deymier sets up her magnificent stall, Brocante&Co, in the village square in Eygalières.

PHAR
Allopathie
Homeopathie
Veterinaire
04 90 95 90 55

CHAPTER 1

Paintings

Antique paintings are devious creatures. You start out buying a small oil on board or charming watercolor, drawn in by the romantic notion of the artist setting out from home on a Sunday afternoon, pitching his folding seat beside an old oak tree and opening his box of paints and brushes to capture the view before him. A few weeks later, you come across another painting that would keep the first company—then another, and another. Before you know it, you have a collection. Friends start commenting on your tastefully grouped displays, and soon you've started venturing into still lifes and portraits. It doesn't take long before there are no more empty walls in your house.

Paintings can have several lives, from the first brushstroke to the finished canvas changing hands through galleries and down generations. You can buy a painting to hang in a hallway, and then after some months, suddenly decide it should move to the dining room. Each setting reveals a new side to the artwork, while the artwork itself transforms the space.

If you're thinking of becoming a regular collector, sourcing is everything. A lucky, chance purchase is always fun, but to grow a collection mindfully it's best to identify dealers with tastes similar to your own. Build up a relationship with sellers who understand your style, and often they will source items with your preferences in mind. Buying at auction can also bring a particular thrill—not only does the buyer need to hunt down and identify the works that interest them, but there is also the competition to be dealt with. Stay focused; the thrill of a bidding war is a clever tactic by the auctioneer—and a good way to lose sight of a carefully planned budget.

Over the years I have often set out to buy antiques in the company of others. It's fun to compare notes and to help each other spot a potential purchase, but one thing I have learned is that beauty is subjective. This is particularly true for art; you have to follow your own taste and instinct, to develop your budding collection with a cohesive style. Researching the art world is therefore time well spent. The more you read, the more you will hone your own eye and judgment. Visiting art museums, reading about the lives of artists, and even taking classes yourself will heighten your appreciation of other artists' work.

For those seeking authoritative reference materials, the *Benezit Dictionary of Artists* is an invaluable resource. It details biographical and market information on thousands of painters and sculptors, and can be used to better understand the aesthetic value and provenance of your acquisitions.

A framed canvas from the nineteenth century sets the scene for a display complete with medici urns at Stéphane Olivier in Paris.

French Art Movements

While most antique paintings you'll encounter are from the nineteenth and twentieth centuries, when starting a collection, it's useful to familiarize yourself with the key French art styles. Artists often reference one another and build on past movements, so understanding these styles will help you place your finds within a broader historical and stylistic context.

Below are distinguishing characteristics of notable art movements in France that you're likely to come across while antiquing:

FACING PAGE
A fine eighteenth-century portrait is hung above a carved wooden console at Yveline Antiques on Place Furstemberg in Paris.

ABOVE, LEFT
This eighteenth-century Italian cityscape is showcased in an unusual oval frame.

ABOVE, RIGHT
A French eighteenth-century oil painting depicting a young girl holding a posy of flowers.

Gothic (1150–1500)

Dominated by religious themes, Gothic paintings are characterized by elongated figures, intricate detailing, rich color palettes, and plenty of gold leaf. Panel paintings, illuminated manuscripts, and frescoes were the primary mediums of this era.

Renaissance (1500–1600)

French artists adopted the Italian approach to perspective, with realistic proportions. Oil painting became favored over tempera (pigmented egg wash), with a focus on portraiture and classical themes.

Baroque (1600–1720)

Artists introduced dramatic lighting and intense emotion into their compositions, often depicting religious and mythological subjects with a sense of grandeur.

Neoclassicism (1780–1820)

This movement emerged as a reaction against baroque and rococo frivolity. Artists returned to classical ideals of symmetry and order, focusing on formal compositions and heroic narratives.

Romanticism (1820–1850)

Romanticism in painting emphasized emotion, drama, and movement, often depicting turbulent scenes in rich, dynamic compositions.

Realism (1840–1880)

Artists started to reject idealization, favoring raw observation and an unembellished portrayal of everyday life. Often somber in tone and subject matter, and featuring loose brushstrokes, this movement marked the beginning of a turn away from the principles of classical art.

ABOVE, LEFT
An imposing portrait of a nobleman dating from the eighteenth century, possibly of Italian origin.

ABOVE, RIGHT
Nineteenth-century portraits are easy to source and make great statement pieces.

ABOVE, LEFT
An early twentieth-century portrait of a card player.

ABOVE, RIGHT
A fragment of a mythological painting is arranged alongside nineteenth-century confit pots and eighteenth-century books.

Impressionism (1860–1890)

Characterized by loose, visible brushstrokes and vibrant colors, impressionist paintings were often executed outdoors, *en plein air*. Impressionists captured the natural world and scenes of leisure, aiming to evoke a sense of immediacy and atmosphere.

Pointillism (1884–1910)

Pointillist artists used the science of color theory to apply tiny, precise dots of contrasting pigment to create optical illusions of luminosity. A notable feature of many pointillist artworks: a painted border—almost like a frame within the frame—designed to complement the artwork and play with its edges.

Post-impressionism (1885–1910)

Building on impressionism's use of color and light, post-impressionist artworks feature structure, emotion, and symbolism, often using bold colors, exaggerated forms, and experimental techniques. This period gave rise to movements such as fauvism, which embraced non-naturalistic color, and cubism, which manipulated perspective and form.

French Schools of Art

Neither formal institutions nor defined movements, the French *écoles* were loose collectives of artists who worked closely together or were drawn to the same region. They often shared techniques, themes, and the culture and visual motifs of the local surroundings—even if they didn't follow a single doctrine or teacher. While each artist in a given school will have their individual style, their work collectively reflects a shared sensibility or moment in time.

École de Barbizon (1830–1870)

The Barbizon school was instrumental in the shift toward naturalism, emerging from a group of artists working in the small village of Barbizon, near the Fontainebleau forest. Their focus on landscapes and rural scenes laid the groundwork for impressionism, emphasizing direct observation and the changing effects of light. Notable artists from this group include Jean-François Millet and Charles-François Daubigny.

École de Bretagne (1850–1930)

Drawn to Brittany's rugged coastline and distinctive light, artists began visiting the region in the mid-nineteenth century to sketch scenes of rural life. The movement gathered momentum in the 1880s and 1890s, particularly around Pont-Aven, where Paul Gauguin and others developed a bold, symbolic style. It continued into the early twentieth century, with painters often depicting the region's customs and wild, windswept landscapes.

École de Paris (1900–1940)

An international group of post-impressionist artists working in Paris—particularly Montparnasse—who blended fauvism, cubism, and expressionism. Their emotional and intense works captured the city's avant-garde energy, pushing the boundaries of modern art in the early twentieth century. The circle included artists such as Amedeo Modigliani, Marc Chagall, and Jules Pascin.

A selection of small framed oil paintings just waiting to be sorted and displayed.

The Collector's Eye

When beginning an art collection, start small and immediately hang or display the pieces in your home. As the collection expands, your eye will naturally develop a sense of which works complement one another and which deserve to stand alone. Over time, you'll also become more adept at recognizing quality, condition, and authenticity.

When considering an oil painting, examine the surface carefully. Is the paint evenly applied, or are there areas where the canvas shows through unintentionally? Look closely for any *manques*—small chips in the paint—along with any visible cracks, distortions, or evidence of overpainting. Has the canvas been relined or restored? Signs of repair can indicate either careful conservation or an attempt to mask damage. None of these alterations make the painting worthless, but they should be noted and taken into account when buying or negotiating a purchase.

Watercolors and pastels are particularly tempting, their delicate nature lending nuance to a collection. However, they are almost always sold framed behind glass, which makes assessing their condition, as well as shipping, more complex. If possible, examine the work outside of its frame. Watch for signs of foxing (small brown spots caused by oxidation) or warping from moisture exposure.

It's always a bonus to purchase a painting bearing the artist's signature. The name may be totally unknown, or it may allow for the piece to be identified as part of an artist's body of work. Either way, it adds another level of understanding, providing welcome information to the art connoisseur thirsty to know more. While some artists sign only on the front (either the full name or just the surname), others inscribe their name, date, or even a dedication on the back. Nevertheless, it's useful to note that signing a painting is a relatively recent phenomenon. The practice gained popularity among some of the great artists of the Renaissance—the most obvious being Leonardo da Vinci—but only became widespread in the nineteenth century.

Lastly, always inspect the frame, as it can reveal a great deal about a painting's history, condition, and value. Up to the nineteenth century, picture frames were always wooden, with carved details, and occasionally gilded with gold leaf. From the nineteenth century onward, ornate frames were made more economically, using plaster molds applied to a wooden base. Sadly, these plaster details become fragile with time, and may chip or crack. They can be repaired by an expert, or at home with a good deal of patience. Older frames are also constructed with mitered, hand-jointed corners, often secured with wooden pegs or nails. More recent frames, by contrast, tend to be stapled or glued. If the back of a frame is covered with a uniform sheet of brown paper, it may suggest a modern mounting.

An eclectic mix of nineteenth-century portraits and landscapes at Fannette Wallerand's store in Rouen.

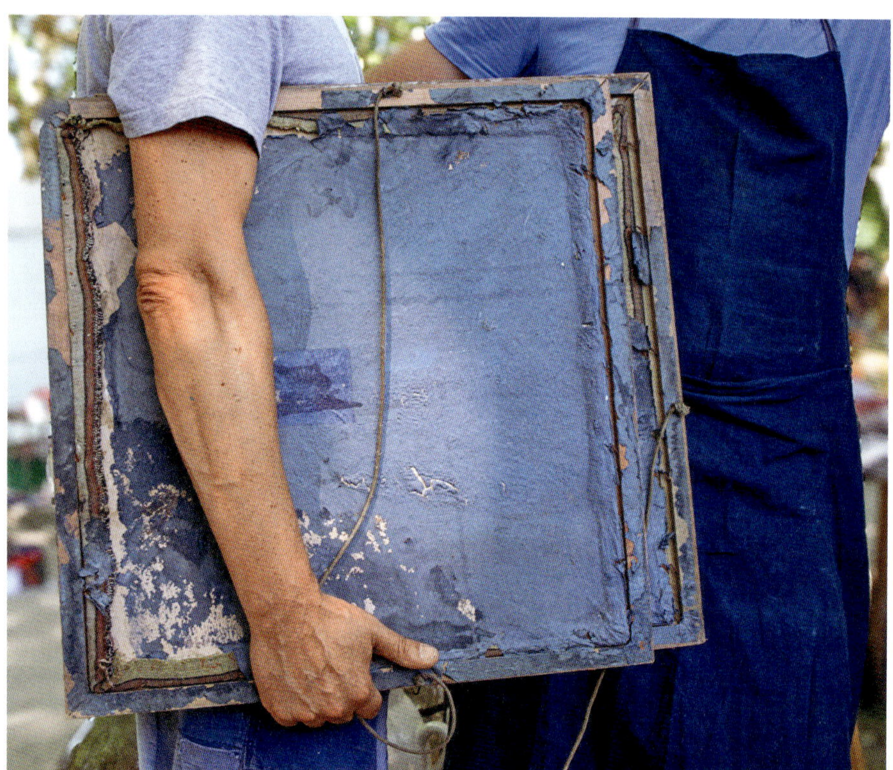

Caring for Antique Paintings

Frames should typically remain with their artworks, as they are part of the piece's history, and are valuable in their own right. A trusted framer can offer invaluable advice and expertise in how to highlight your art to its best advantage. For unframed paintings, you'll want to protect the edges by lining your chosen frame with foam or rubber strips, or velvet. If the frame is too deep, cork strips can be used to pad it out. For artworks on paper—whether paintings or prints—it's essential to mount them on acid-free board to prevent deterioration. A mount can also be used to keep the artwork from touching the glass.

When hanging your artwork, avoid direct sunlight and damp, and never position it above a fireplace or radiator, as heat can quickly cause damage. Rather than placing a painting flush against the wall, allow it to lean slightly outward from the top, to improve air circulation. Hanging art in kitchens and bathrooms can pose particular challenges as humidity can fluctuate greatly. If displaying art in these rooms, avoid paper-based works, use a sealed frame, and ensure the space is well ventilated.

When handling a painting, always use clean, dry hands and touch only the frame to avoid transferring oils onto the surface. When it comes to cleaning, less is more. A gentle dusting with a soft brush once or twice a year is enough. If it requires deeper cleaning or restoration, always entrust the job to a professional.

ABOVE
Buyers instinctively conceal their purchases when walking through a fair, protecting them from physical damage and prying eyes.

FACING PAGE
At the Puces de Vanves, some dealers display their wares in a casual manner. Here, an oil on board is propped against a tree on the sidewalk.

PAGE 32
A painting by artist Renée Carpentier-Wintz, who lived in Brittany and loved painting marine scenes.

PAGE 33
A portrait of Breton girls by Sophie Morisse.

PAGES 34–35
A large selection of unframed oil paintings on board.

SOCIETE ALGER

MEET THE EXPERT

Yves Berger

Galerie du Crabe
Granville, Normandy
@lecrabedegranville

YVES'S TIPS

Above all, Yves emphasizes the importance of a good frame. Believing the wrong frame can ruin an artwork, he often reframes the works he displays to complement the strengths of each painting. His advice for buyers: "First and foremost, buy what you love and trust your instinct. If you are looking to collect seriously, then pay attention to the painter's name, and don't hesitate to include artists that are already known.
If a painting is damaged, show it to a professional restorer before trying any homemade remedies. And, most of all, enjoy your collection. Display it in your home and move paintings around to see them in different lights. A collection has to live and evolve to be worthwhile."

For over twenty years, Yves Berger has been buying and selling art in Granville, a coastal town in Normandy that ranks just behind Honfleur for its wealth of galleries and antique dealers. He began his career as a writer, but a fascination with old books and their illustrations gradually drew him into the world of art.

Today, writing is still a love, but antique paintings are his specialty, and his gallery carries a fine selection of landscapes, portraits, illustrations, and marine scenes. In addition to welcoming clients at his Normandy store, Yves is a regular seller at the famous Chatou fair, which is held twice annually near Paris, and he can also be found at the Rouen antique fair. He spends much of his time on the road purchasing art for his business, though he rarely sources from auctions or *déballages*. Instead, he relies on the network he has built up over the years, which supplies him with plenty of opportunities to buy art directly from estate sales and private sources.

Yves's clients appreciate his in-depth knowledge of the artists he carries, dictated by his personal taste. Although he often shows several pieces by the same name, he maintains that a painting has to speak to or move him in some way before he adds it to his roster. Originally hailing from Brittany, he has a particular affection for the École de Bretagne.

CHAPTER 2

Books, Illustrations, and Ephemera

Buying antique books is about far more than collecting pages of interesting content. While there are talented dealers who seek out centuries-old leather-bound volumes, or rare first editions for a specialized public, this is not the only source or reason for buying and selling antique books.

Perhaps nothing speaks of refinement quite like a library lined with leather-bound books. In eighteenth- and nineteenth-century France, books were typically bound in calfskin, goatskin (known as morocco), or sheepskin, often with gilt edges, marbled endpapers, and intricate spine detailing. Some bindings feature gold tooling, raised bands, and inlays of contrasting leather. Others may include the personal crest or initials of a former owner, adding a biographical element to the book's history.

While some collectors focus on first editions or specific subjects—literature, philosophy, travel, religion—others are drawn to the aesthetic of matching sets. Rows of gold-titled spines in deep red or forest green lend a certain warmth and gravitas to any interior, whether a formal library, a quiet study, or a curated living room.

In interior design, bookshelves and libraries have served as inspiration for decades. Dealers still sell books by the yard to suit a particular palette or mood—whether rows of leather spines, clothbound editions, or pale-hued paperbacks in white, blush, or blue. While trends may shift, books remain a timeless accent.

Suitable for every space and available in every style, antique books whisper of a time when the printed word was both an intellectual and tactile treasure. With their handmade paper, elegant typefaces, marbled or domino endpapers, and the occasional handwritten note or pressed flower between their pages, antique books bring us closer to the world in which they were made. Perhaps that's why they remain so beloved by collectors—inviting us to uncover centuries of learning, artistry, and cultural evolution.

Blue paperbound books add a striking touch of color to a wall display.

baromètre enregistreur
Graphique tracé par

Charançons
LE MORSE
Clairon
Pl. 222
Fig. 3. Le Ganga.
Fig. 4. La Gélinotte des rivages.
Histoire Naturelle

Illustrated Encyclopedias

Some antique books are standouts due to their illustrations. One of the most important projects of the eighteenth century was the creation of the *Encyclopédie*, edited by Denis Diderot and Jean le Rond d'Alembert. Published in several volumes between 1751 and 1772, the *Encyclopédie* was a revolutionary effort to gather and disseminate human knowledge. Lavishly illustrated with thousands of engravings, it covered everything from shipbuilding to textile manufacturing, anatomy to zoology. A full set of the original books is rare and commands a high price, but even owning a single illustrated page is a feat among collectors.

Botanical Illustration

In the late eighteenth century and early nineteenth century, as exploration brought new discoveries to a curious public, illustration flourished, with images of flora and fauna that were both scientifically rigorous and visually arresting. These engravings—once bound in volumes—are now sought after as standalone artworks. The following are among the most celebrated botanical illustrators.

Georges-Louis Leclerc, Comte de Buffon (1707–1788)

Naturalist, mathematician, and cosmologist, Buffon directed the Jardin des Plantes in Paris and published thirty-six quarto volumes of his *Histoire Naturelle* during his lifetime (even more of his research was released posthumously). Often called the father of natural history in France, his vivid illustrations of animals, plants, and landscapes capture the extraordinary nature of expedition and discovery in this era.

Pierre-Joseph Redouté (1759–1840)

Known as the "Raphael of flowers" by his contemporaries, Redouté is perhaps the most recognizable botanical illustrator of all time. His work for Empress Joséphine, including *Les Liliacées* and *Les Roses*, set the standard for botanical art: finely rendered, with delicate use of color.

François-André Michaux (1770–1855)

A French botanist and explorer, Michaux documented North American trees in a monumental work, *Histoire des arbres forestiers de l'Amérique septentrionale*. His illustrations are admired for their rich detail and bold touch.

Pancrace Bessa (1772–1835)

A contemporary and collaborator of Redouté, Bessa's works were often used in luxury botanical publications. His delicate, luminous style is instantly recognizable.

Eighteenth-century illustrations from the Panckoucke encyclopedia are often framed and exhibited as wall hangings.

Special Editions

By the nineteenth and twentieth centuries, illustration took on a new life as leading creatives began merging literature and visual art in unexpected ways. This gave rise to two distinct, though sometimes overlapping, traditions: the commercial *édition de luxe* (luxury edition) and the more avant-garde *livre d'artiste* (artist's book). Though different in tone, both transformed books into works of art. Once aimed at a niche audience—many left languishing in studios or storerooms—these volumes are now among the most collectible and coveted on the market.

Éditions de luxe

Lavishly produced and typically released in limited runs by prestigious publishers, these luxury editions paired fine literature with commissioned illustrations. They were beautifully printed on handmade paper, bound in decorative covers, and often signed by both author and artist. Collaborations such as Pablo Picasso and Paul Éluard's *Le Visage de la Paix*, or Salvador Dalí's surrealist drawings for Michel de Montaigne's essays, merged poetic clarity with bold, modernist images. These books were made to be read, admired, displayed, and treasured.

Livres d'artiste

More radical in spirit, artist's books pushed beyond the traditional bounds of publishing. Created through collaborations between painters, poets, and printers, these books were radical experiments in form, texture, and layout. Henri Matisse, for instance, acted as author, illustrator, and calligrapher of *Jazz*, a vibrant exploration of color, rhythm, and handwritten text. Others, like Joan Miró, Sonia Delaunay, and Salvador Dalí, lent their visual language to volumes by poets and philosophers, creating playful one-of-a-kind creations and limited editions.

ABOVE
Pages from a botanical reference book describing floral varieties in detail.

FACING PAGE
Classical eighteenth-century engravings from the Panckoucke encyclopedia.

PAGES 42 AND 43
Mike Sajnoski combines handwritten documents with antique prints that he has collected over the years.

Fig. 2.
Fig. 6.
Fig. 7.
Fig. 3.
Fig. 8.
Fig. 5.
Fig. 1.
Fig. 4.
ANTIQUITÉS.

MEET THE EXPERT

Mike Sajnoski

The Foraged Studio
Eygalières, Provence
mikesajnoski.com
@mike_sajnoski

It is not easy to define exactly what Mike Sajnoski creates in his studio amid the hills of Provence, but that's part of the intrigue. A seasoned *brocanteur*, Mike deals in all manner of antique finds, yet his true specialty lies in something altogether more imaginative: assembling nineteenth-century illustrations and artworks into layered, mixed-media compositions that feel both timeless and entirely new.

His work blends myriad materials sourced from the region's abundant flea markets—the markets at L'Isle-sur-la-Sorgue, Carpentras, Avignon, and Montpellier are among his favorite haunts. Chandelier crystals, thick gilt frames, botanical prints, scraps of sheet music, fragments of printed text, dried plants, and medicine labels all find their way into his studio. Sometimes these objects are curated into mounted art objects and left to speak for themselves; other times, they are arranged around central figures, incised from other artworks, creating portraits that feel both familiar and fantastical.

Each piece is unique in shape, style, and scale, with frames often layered or reassembled from salvaged wood and glass. Nothing is wasted. Offcuts from furniture he restores are incorporated as sculptural elements or textural backdrops.

Mike's creations—alongside a trove of other curiosities—can be seen by appointment in his studio near Eygalières, or found at the Saturday market in Villeneuve-lès-Avignon and the monthly Sunday *brocante* in Eygalières.

MIKE'S TIPS

Sometimes it helps to go to antique markets with a friend whose taste differs from yours—you'll find things you might otherwise have overlooked. With a bit of imagination, even the most unassuming object can be transformed into something worth treasuring.

Gabriel de Mariquan
Ile de Merens

Parseval

Cachet Mis Frédéric de Parseval

Julien Barbedien

Hélène Bizot Rondot

Régnier Philarète Chasles Ministre du

The Collector's Eye

The value of old books isn't just sentimental. Factors like historical significance, the author's reputation, and even the book's physical components contribute hugely to its collectability.

While first editions tend to be the most desirable, especially if they mark the debut of a major author or work, they're not the only gems out there. Limited editions (with a set, and often numbered, print run), signed copies, early reprints from notable presses, and books featuring illustrations by celebrated artists are well worth seeking out, and make an excellent foundation for a collection—it helps to become familiar with publisher details and printing histories. Books with interesting backstories, such as those containing a discreet bookplate, an inscription from the author, or a known history of ownership, can also carry special weight for collectors.

Leather-bound volumes with decorative tooling, books with marbled or gilt edges, endpapers with custom artwork, or covers with embossed lettering tend to be more collectable. Some people look for matched sets, others for unique bindings. These details make all the difference when you live with your books as objects, not just texts.

However beautiful a binding, it is only part of the picture. Books with intact spines, clean pages, and minimal damage from moisture or insects not only look better, but will be easier to care for. A bit of foxing (those small brown specks), gentle fading, or softening of the corners is normal—and even part of the charm—but avoid anything too brittle to handle.

Completeness is another factor to consider. Check to see if a book contains all its pages, illustrations, and any accompanying materials. Hand-colored engravings, maps, etchings, or early lithographs can elevate a book's value considerably. For books sold by the set, check that all the volumes are included, or if there were any other titles originally present in the collection.

Finally, follow your curiosity. Whether it's natural history, old cookbooks, or slim volumes of poetry that catch your eye, let your interests lead the way. And remember, there's an entire universe of antique ephemera to explore beyond the bookshelf. You might find yourself drawn to early postcards, embossed letterheads, elegant handwritten merchant ledgers, block-printed domino paper, or hotel stationery that speaks of another time. Pay attention, and patterns and affinities for certain subjects or eras will emerge in your collecting habits, often revealing where your own specialty might naturally take shape.

Handwritten envelopes with wax seals impart a romantic air.

Caring for Books and Ephemera

Particularly susceptible to discoloration and foxing, antique books and papers require careful handling to preserve their beauty and longevity. Always use clean, dry hands, and, when removing a book from a shelf, avoid tugging from the top of its spine. Instead, gently press the volumes on either side and remove the book by holding both edges of the spine. Try not to open older books too widely, as this can stress and crease the spine. Maintain a modest opening angle and avoid placing books face down. You may consider investing in a specialist book support for reading or display. Turn pages from the corner, rather than inserting a finger halfway along the page and risking a tear.

Books and works on paper appreciate a dry, stable environment, away from direct sunlight, which can fade bindings and illustrations. Good airflow also helps keep mildew at bay, while a steady temperature and low humidity prevent warping. A quick rule of thumb: if a room feels pleasant to you, chances are your books will be comfortable there as well.

When storing or displaying your collection, avoid overcrowding your shelves, which can put too much pressure on book covers. Instead, arrange books evenly, grouping similar sizes together and keeping them upright to help prevent warping. Particularly tall or fragile volumes are better stored flat—just not in teetering stacks. A vitrine or bookcase with glass doors is ideal for reducing dust buildup, though regular gentle dusting with a soft brush or cloth will suffice.

If you do discover damage, resist the urge to repair loose pages or fraying bindings with household tape, glue, or elastic bands; these can cause discoloration and leave damaging residue. Instead, secure loose books temporarily with cotton tape or a strip of scrap fabric until they can be seen by a professional conservator for proper restoration.

If you'd like to frame an antique illustration, choose acid-free, archival-quality materials for mounting. Avoid frames that are sealed too tightly, as trapped moisture can cause damage over time. Similarly, steer clear of heavy, metal components that might corrode and leave marks. If you're rotating pieces, store unused illustrations flat in acid-free folders or archival boxes, with soft tissue between each sheet to protect the surface.

FACING PAGE
In the eighteenth and early nineteenth centuries, books were bound to order, and many remain in their unbound state.

PAGE 48
An eighteenth-century world atlas showing a map of China and the Indies by Italian cartographer Giovanni Rizzi Zannoni.

PAGE 49
Leatherbound legal volumes, grouped by year of publication.

PAGES 50–51
Books from the Bible bound individually and titled by hand.

histoire du peuple de dieu
histoire du peuple de dieu
EN présence

MER GLACIALE
d'Aral
Samarkand
TARTARIE INDÉPENDANTE
TARTARIE CHINOISE
la Grande Muraille
PERSE
MOGOL ou INDOSTAN
INDE
G.de Cambaye
Amedabad
Surate
Bombay
Chaul
Delhi
Bouche du Gange
GOLFE DE BENGALE
Dalai Lama
Pekin
G.de Petcheli
CHAN-TON
HONAN
CHEN-SI
Nankin
KIAN-NAN
HU-QUANG
KIANG-SI
QUANTON
Macao
I.Formose
Tayoan
ISLES LEQUEO
Tropique du Cancer
Haynan
Sinhoa
COCHINCHINE
Pracel
Martaban
Nicobar
Andaman
I.de CEILAN
Maldives
Achem
Equateur
ISLES DE LA SONDE
Banca
Borneo
Java
Materam
Madura
Macassar
Manille
Samar ou Tendaye
ISLES MOLUQUES
N.GUINÉE
Timorland
Timor
OCÉAN ORIENTAL
CORÉE
CHINE,
INDES

MEET THE EXPERT

Marc Razé

L'Armillaire Ancienne
Évreux, Normandy
armillaireancienne.com
@armillaireancienne_oldbooks

Having worked in the world of antique books for decades, Mark Razé is one of the rare French dealers who can supply to order. Be it an original copy of Diderot and Alembert's *Encyclopédie*, a collection of illustrations by Buffon, or an eighteenth-century atlas, Marc finds a way to source it for his clients.

Although he has no physical store, his clientele of collectors is regular and faithful. They trust his discerning eye, and are happy to buy directly online, or to travel to see him when he shows at the antique fairs of Rouen, Chatou, and Compiègne, as well as at the antique salon at Saint-Méloir-des-Ondes, which takes place in Brittany in August. It is also possible to visit his premises, by appointment only.

Above all, Marc understands the beauty of books, and the pleasure of a book-lined room. He specializes in complete sets of leather-bound volumes, and even offers unbound eighteenth-century texts, which offer a different appeal. When dealing in antique illustrations, he will sometimes commission a watercolorist to painstakingly paint a set of botanical or natural-history prints by hand, enhancing the existing beauty of the fine-lined drawing.

MARC'S TIPS

While complete volumes are undeniably striking, don't overlook the impact of a single illustrated page. Thoughtfully hand-colored or framed with dignity, it can hold its own and draw the eye in unexpected ways.

Prudhomme
Revolutions
de
Paris.

CHAPTER 3

Silver Tableware

There is something very special about setting a table with antique silverware. Beyond the gleam of polished metal, there is a real sense of creating everyday magic, adding both beauty to the table and enjoyment to the meal.

I have clear memories of my parents using silverware at the table for their dinner parties. There was always a sense of ceremony when the table was set, and just as much care was taken beforehand to polish each piece until it shone. It was a small effort, but one that marked the occasion as something special.

Antique silverware, or *argenterie ancienne*, is far more than a decorative detail. It tells us how people dined, entertained, and expressed refinement through the objects around them. From the ornate rococo curves of eighteenth-century spoons to the streamlined elegance of 1930s art deco cutlery, these pieces offer a glimpse into France's shifting tastes and the dining rituals that brought them to life.

Of all the items laid on a French dining table, silver has perhaps the most storied past. Long regarded as a symbol of prestige, it played a central role in dining, particularly among the aristocracy. As early as the seventeenth century, under the ancien régime, the nobility commissioned elaborate sets of silver flatware to reflect their status. Dining became almost theatrical, with each course calling for a different utensil: oyster forks, sorbet spoons, marrow scoops—the list goes on.

By the nineteenth century, silver flatware had become a fixture in the bourgeois home, often presented in a fitted case—known as a *ménagère*—as a wedding gift or family heirloom. And while fully laying a table in silver may no longer be in vogue, classic silverware patterns such as Perles, Filet, Rocaille, and Rubans remain as beloved by families and collectors today as they were in centuries past. These enduring designs are still produced by the great houses, with certain names particularly prized among antique enthusiasts.

Les Tables d'Eva at the Puces de Saint-Ouen boasts an impressive collection of silver tableware for dining and entertaining in style.

Silverware Houses

Christofle (1830–present)

Perhaps the most internationally recognized name in French silverware, Christofle revolutionized silver-plating techniques and made elegant tableware accessible to a broader audience without compromising on quality. Pieces made before 1935 have a hallmark featuring a set of scales, while those produced after 1935 typically bear a knight's head.

Puiforcat (1820–present)

Known for its exceptional craftsmanship and distinctive neoclassical aesthetic, Puiforcat has long been a favorite among connoisseurs. The house is now part of the Hermès group and continues to produce both historically inspired and contemporary pieces. Many of its designs have a sculptural quality, with particular attention paid to weight and proportion in the hand.

Odiot (1690–present)

One of the oldest and most prestigious names in French silverware, Odiot was once the official silversmith to Napoleon and the imperial court. Its pieces reflect this legacy: they are richly decorated, often grand in scale, and unmistakably regal. Empire motifs such as eagles, bees, and laurel wreaths feature prominently in its work.

Ercuis (1867–present)

Slightly more modern in spirit, Ercuis has established a reputation for silverware with clean lines and discreet ornamentation. Antique sets, particularly from the belle époque and art deco periods, are particularly prized for their balanced proportions and quiet elegance. The house's modern lines are often found in luxury hotels and fine restaurants, and aboard high-end cruise liners.

Boulenger (1810–c. 1930s)

Although no longer active, Boulenger was a major player in the late nineteenth and early twentieth centuries, and was known for its refined tableware, crisp art nouveau lines, and large-scale production. Boulenger's silver graced the tables of the French Navy and famed luxury liners such as the SS *Normandie*, winning numerous medals at global exhibitions. The house closed in the late 1930s, but its silver and silver plate—particularly flatware—remain highly collectible for their craftsmanship and stylistic range.

François Frionnet (twentieth century)

This silversmith is known for sterling silver cutlery produced mainly between the 1930s and 1970s. Mostly art deco and mid-century in style, its work features clean lines and geometric detailing, but a few sets revive *rocaille* and Louis XV designs. Pieces are durable, weighty, and streamlined, with mid-century blades, often in stainless steel, and handles in silver plate. More substantial than Christofle, they make an excellent choice for everyday dining.

Vintage Christofle flatware can often be found complete with its original packaging.

Orfèvre à Paris depuis 1830
MAD
Christofle
Christofle
Orfèvre à Paris depuis 1830

Popular Styles

Perles

Introduced by Christofle in the late nineteenth century, *perles* draws on the neoclassical taste of the Louis XVI era. Pieces are delicately bordered with beading, inspired by rows of pearls. This remains one of Christofle's most enduring patterns.

Filet

Emerging in eighteenth-century France, *filet* is defined by its raised threadlike border that follows the shape of the handle. Adopted by houses such as Puiforcat, Ercuis, and Christofle, it embodies classical restraint and quiet authority—and remains a constant favorite on French tables.

Rocaille

Taking its name from the rococo movement, *rocaille* is lavish and sculptural, with scrolling shells and ornamental curves. It was particularly popular among nineteenth-century makers such as Odiot and Boulenger, who revived the style with gusto.

Rubans

Adorned with ribbons and bows, this style embraces the femininity of late eighteenth-century French design. Christofle's version, introduced in the early 1900s, remains the most recognizable, although similar motifs appear throughout French flatware from this period.

FACING PAGE
The traditional boxes used for flatware are known as *menagères*.

ABOVE
French and English silver plate knives on display in L'Isle-sur-la-Sorgue.

MEET THE EXPERTS

Maurice and Patricia di Matteo

Reassort & Couverts
Champagne
ebay.fr/str/reassortcouvert
@reassortcouverts

Maurice and Patricia di Matteo share a deep passion for tablescapes, particularly where silverware is concerned. Until twenty years ago, Maurice worked in hospitality, and there's little he doesn't know about entertaining and creating a beautiful table setting.

Together, they are France's foremost specialists in antique and vintage Christofle tableware, and experts in restoring antique silverware, which they refurbish in their atelier, located in the Champagne region. Batches of cutlery arrive tarnished and worn, but after hours of meticulous work, they reemerge gleaming—and highly coveted.

What began as a personal venture has since grown into a larger operation. They now work with scouts across France, sourcing silverware both for specific orders and to assemble a broad inventory for their regular clients.

Although their atelier is in the Champagne region, Maurice and Patricia sell their restored silverware online and at antique fairs around Paris. Connoisseurs looking for special tableware or unique gifts know that this is the place to find extraordinary pieces.

MAURICE AND PATRICIA'S TIPS

Be inventive about how you use antique pieces. Serving forks with finger guards may no longer be customary at the table, but they make perfect grilling tools at summer barbecues. If you fall in love with a piece, imagine how it might serve you in more than one way. And if it's no longer in fashion—no matter. Mix and match, or simply display it.

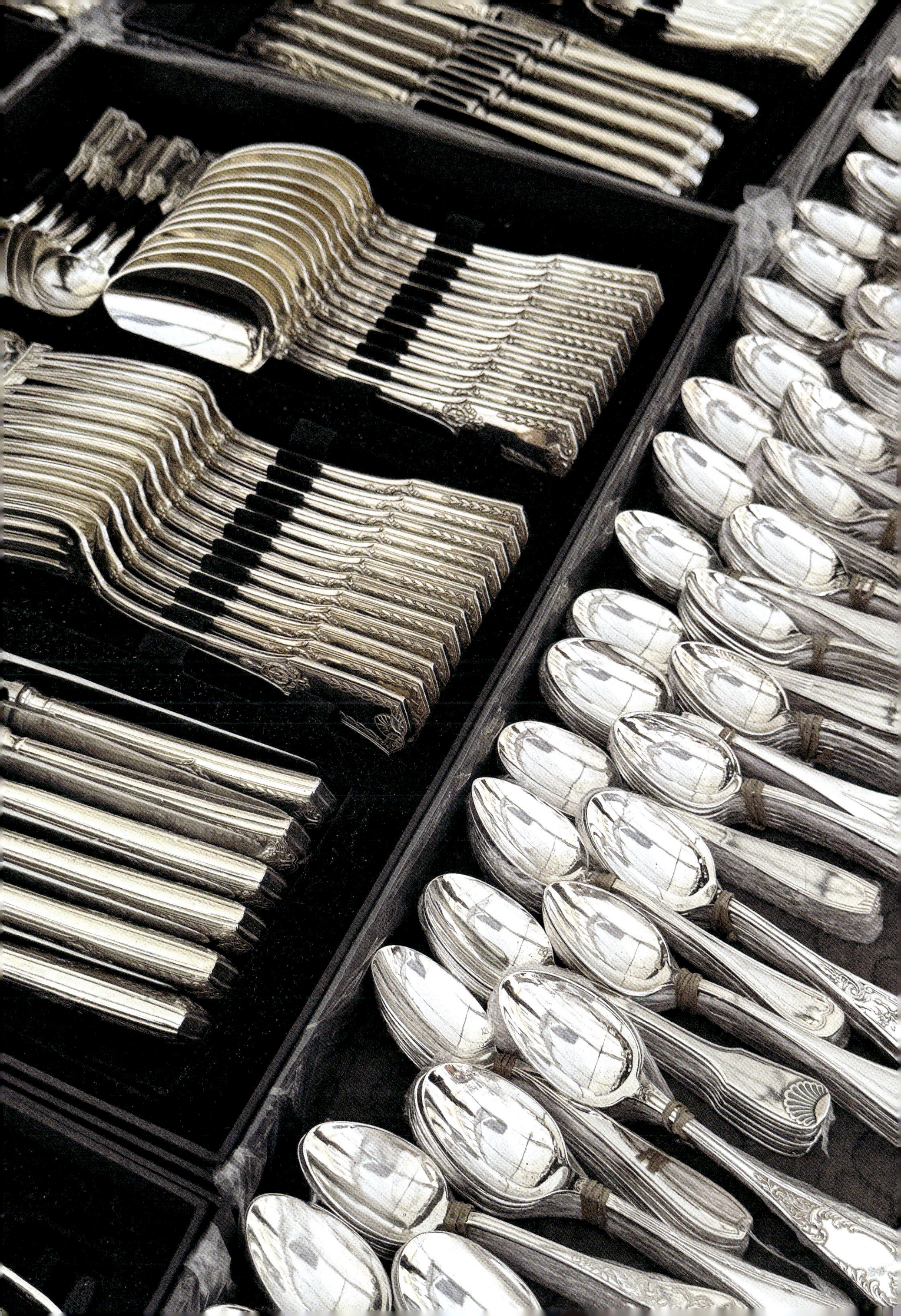

The Collector's Eye

French silverware is a pleasure to use and to collect, but only if you understand what you're holding. Whether you're assembling a full service or simply selecting a few special pieces, it is essential to know how to recognize quality.

The first distinction is material. Solid sterling silver, known as *argent massif*, contains at least 95 percent pure silver. It's heavy in the hand, softens to a warm patina over time, and is always hallmarked. Silver plate, by contrast, is a thin layer of silver over a base metal like nickel or copper. It's lighter, more affordable, and lovely for occasional use, though it will wear more quickly. For frequent entertainers or long-term collectors, sterling is a worthwhile investment. But a table laid with well-made silver plate is just as elegant—and perhaps involves less worry about scratches.

Hallmarks are your guide. French silver is rigorously marked, and learning to read these tiny stamps makes collecting far more rewarding. The most important is the Minerva head: a profile of the Roman goddess framed in an octagon, introduced in 1838. The number inside her helmet indicates purity: "1" for 950/1000 silver (sterling) or "2" for 800/1000 silver (lower grade). Alongside this you'll usually find a maker's mark—a lozenge or diamond shape bearing the silversmith's initials and symbol—which can be cross-checked in hallmark guides. Pieces prior to the French Revolution may have marks such as crowned letters, animals, or city symbols; these are less standardized, but fascinating nonetheless. Plated pieces don't bear the Minerva; instead, look for house marks or numbers indicating the silver weight used in the plating process.

A good magnifying glass—or, even better, a jeweler's loupe—is invaluable when examining antique silver, paired with a trusted reference guide. If you're uncertain of origin, take the time to conduct some research before buying. Reputable vendors will usually offer close-up photographs and should be willing to answer questions or provide documentation if asked.

It is also necessary to assess the feel of silverware. Quality silver is well balanced and pleasantly weighty. A fork or spoon should rest easily in the hand, without feeling flimsy or sharp-edged. Patterns should be crisp and detailed, not rubbed smooth by time. A polished surface can disguise flaws, so inspect pieces in natural light, paying careful attention to fork tines, spoon bowls, and knife handles: are they evenly worn, or do they show signs of heavy use or repair? Minor dings or surface scratches are acceptable, but look closely for signs of soldering, deep pitting, or silver plate that has been worn down to the base metal.

While sets in pristine condition may seem tempting, they are likely to be modern reproductions—true antiques usually bear the gentle marks of use. That said, there's no need to hold out for a complete service. If you're just beginning, start small. A few mismatched dessert spoons or a beautifully monogrammed server can impart charm and personality to your table. In time, these individual finds may evolve into a collection that will feel all the more personal for having been gathered piece by piece.

PAGE 58
A complete dinner set of Christofle Louis XV Marly design silverware.

PAGE 59
Silver plate flatware by Chambly in Sans Gene design.

FACING PAGE
Nineteenth-century English tea and coffee pots, and water jug.

Caring for Antique Silverware

Many collectors are reluctant to use their silverware, lest it be damaged. But silver is surprisingly resilient, and these pieces were designed to be used, developing a natural patina over time that only adds to their beauty.

When it comes to cleaning, it's best to handwash with warm water and a mild, unscented dish soap. Avoid citrus-based or strongly fragranced soaps, as these can damage the silver. After washing, dry the pieces immediately to prevent water spots and tarnishing. Never soak silverware, especially silver-plated items, as this can cause the metal to separate from its base. Note that acidic foods like eggs, lemon, mustard, or certain fruits, can cause discoloration—avoid serving these foods in your silverware, or wash it immediately after use.

While generally not recommended for most antique silver, the dishwasher can be used for more recent silverware by Christofle, with proper precautions. Before the first use, hand-wash the silverware with a neutral, fragrance-free dish soap. When using the dishwasher, choose a gentle powder detergent free from chlorine and citric acid—avoid gels, liquids, multipurpose tablets, and dishwasher salts, which often contain harsh additives. Silver does not mix well with stainless steel, so always keep them in separate compartments or baskets in the dishwasher. After the cycle, leave the door ajar to let steam escape, and dry any remaining moisture promptly. Do not machine-wash older knives (pre-1968), as their construction may not withstand modern cycles. Be mindful of water hardness, too—excess limescale can corrode silver over time.

When it comes to polishing, less is more. Excessive rubbing can wear away details, particularly on silver-plated items. Instead, use a nonabrasive polish and a soft cloth, focusing on tarnished areas rather than buffing the entire piece. For storage, keep silverware in tarnish-resistant rolls or cloth pouches, laying each piece flat and separately to prevent scratches. To guard against humidity, tuck in a few silica gel packs, especially if storing in a drawer or closed cabinet.

ABOVE
Silver cutlery can be sourced easily, especially if styles are mixed and matched.

FACING PAGE
English and French nineteenth-century dessert spoons and cake forks

PAGE 64
Early twentieth-century spoons in their original boxes.

PAGE 65
Mismatched silver napkin rings of different styles and eras.

PAGES 66–67
In the summer, the façade of Dickinson Antiquities is dressed in foliage.

MEET THE EXPERT

Kate Dickinson

Dickinson Antiquities
L'Isle-sur-la-Sorgue, Provence
dickinsonantiquities.com
@k8silverplate

In a quiet courtyard in one of France's most renowned antique markets, Kate Dickinson's boutique glistens like the treasures within. A specialist in antique silver plate, Kate has become a trusted presence in L'Isle-sur-la-Sorgue, particularly for those seeking refined objects to brighten their table.

Her collection is both extensive and beautifully curated, spanning cutlery, serving utensils, goblets, candlesticks, trays, and other decorative silverware. Each piece is chosen for its craftsmanship and character, and the luster of the collection is matched by the gracious welcome extended to all who visit.

Originally from the UK, Kate and her husband, an antique dealer and restorer, settled in this Provençal village to focus on English silver plate—a category long appreciated in France but difficult to find locally. Today, her stock blends the best of both worlds. She sources many of her pieces from Sheffield, renowned for its craftsmanship, alongside well-known French makers like Christofle. Though she sells some solid silver, it is the silver plate that gives her shop its distinct character, with clients particularly fond of her collection of champagne buckets, trays, cocktail shakers, and silver table bells.

Thanks to a thriving online store, Kate's reach is international, and she regularly ships to customers across the globe, from Spain and Germany to the Philippines and Australia.

KATE'S TIPS

If you like a piece and can afford it—buy it. "So many people come in to browse, then come back two weeks later for something that caught their eye, and it's gone," she says. "They can't get another one and they're disappointed."

DICKINSON ANTIQUIT
DICKINSON
Antiquités

CHAPTER 4

Ceramics, Glass, and Tableware

There is a philosophical debate between those who believe we should save our most precious possessions for special occasions and those who believe we should use them every day, to enjoy their beauty. This is a familiar dilemma when it comes to our wardrobes, but it also applies to antique tableware. Many sets of old porcelain—delicate and often considerably valuable—are relegated to the confines of cupboards, hidden away from sight, preventing their beauty from truly flourishing.

I discovered the world of antique tableware when I began buying regularly at flea markets. Until then, I had assumed antique plates and dishes would be grand and expensive: gilded edges, elaborate hand-painted designs, prestigious names—the kind of items best kept behind glass. I had completely overlooked the huge selection of nineteenth-century transferware (ceramics featuring a design applied by transferring a wet print on paper made from an inked, engraved copper plate to unfired pottery). With their simple floral motifs, these pieces make for beautiful, mix-and-match table settings and are easy to find at fairs. My collection quickly grew.

We often change the plates we use at home—sometimes I'll buy a service, enjoy it for a time, then pass it along to one of the kids or rotate it out for the season. It's a quiet pleasure to mix and match patterns, shapes, and materials; even mismatched services can look beautiful on a considered table. Pieces not in use often find a second life on display. Over time, everyone gravitates toward a style that feels right in the hand and suits the moment.

In France, a refined table setting was once the measure of social status, regional pride, and artistic taste—and in many ways, it still is. In addition to table settings, ceramics and stoneware used elsewhere in the home are equally important. From simple ironstone milk jugs to fabulous vases, there are many styles and eras to choose from. I have a collection of white ironstone tureens, which I like to have on display, while others prefer the bright colors of majolica.

Each piece of ceramic and glassware carries its own sensory character—weight, temperature, texture, translucency—as well as distinct technical demands, which affect their durability and desirability. Designed for many different contexts, the material makeup and provenance of your tableware should be thoroughly understood before you begin considering motif or value. As you explore the following styles and materials, you'll begin to recognize—and refine—what you naturally gravitate toward.

A large collection of eighteenth- and nineteenth-century white ceramics are displayed in L'Isle-sur-la-Sorgue.

Materials

Stoneware

Nonporous and fired at high temperatures for greater strength, ceramics made from this material, known as *grès* in French, are ideal for regular use. Often left unglazed on the exterior, pieces have thick walls, a sturdy feel, and neutral colors.

Hard- and soft-paste porcelain

Porcelain is a highly vitrified ceramic known for its smooth and refined texture. There are two types to choose from. *Porcelaine dure* (hard-paste porcelain, or "true" porcelain) is made from kaolin, feldspar, and quartz, and is fired at high temperatures. It is tough, durable, and resistant to crazing (fine cracks in the glaze), though it can be more brittle at the rims where the porcelain has been shaped. *Porcelaine tendre* (soft-paste porcelain) uses a mix of kaolin and other materials, fired at lower temperatures, resulting in a softer, less durable finish with a warmer texture.

Mixed clay

Often used for nineteenth-century bowls and teapots, *terre mêlée* is produced by marbling together contrasting colored clays to form swirling patterns. Each piece—usually in earthy tones or blue and white, and sometimes unglazed—is one of a kind.

FACING PAGE
A charming assortment of blue-and-white transferware.

ABOVE
In Provence, antique confit pots and ceramics reflect the warm hues of the south.

Faïence

Typically used as decorative pieces today, these ceramics are made of earthenware coated in a distinctive white glaze of tin oxide and lead, designed to mimic the finish of Chinese porcelain, albeit without its translucency. Fired at low temperatures, faïence is relatively fragile, but its vivid designs make it especially prized by collectors.

Glass

Pre-1850 glass can be handblown, mold-blown, or pressed. It may have varying thickness, small bubbles, and, in the case of handblown pieces, punt marks where the piece has been separated from the metal rod (punt or pontil). Slightly wavy to the eye and irregular in the hand, these early pieces lack the perfectly smooth finish of industrial glass and are often tinted green, blue, or amethyst due to mineral impurities.

Crystal

Made from a combination of glass and at least 24 percent lead oxide, crystal glassware is heavier and more brilliant than traditional glass. Deep-cut patterns, engraved initials, or etched crests are common features, especially in pieces by prestigious makers, such as Baccarat, Saint-Louis, and Daum. When tapped, crystal produces a clear, resonant ring.

ABOVE, LEFT
A blue-and-white bird plate by Longwy featuring the Mésange design.

ABOVE, RIGHT
A nineteenth-century water jug bears the monogram of its original owner.

FACING PAGE
Nineteenth-century French liqueur glasses, and a decanter repurposed as an attractive vase.

POUDRE

FACING PAGE
Two Longwy plates featuring birds and irises, three Gien plates with Oiseaux-Mouches designs, and three Gien plates decorated with the floral Mai pattern.

ABOVE, LEFT
A polychrome Choisy-le-Roi dinner service.

ABOVE, RIGHT
A selection of pieces featuring the Gien Fuchsia motif, a Pexonne Églantine sauce boat, pieces by Sarreguemines in the Favori pattern, and plates by Sarreguemines with the Fontanges design.

Regional Styles

Rouen (Normandy)

The city of Rouen, in Normandy, has been a center of faïence production since at least the 1540s, with its golden age spanning the seventeenth to nineteenth centuries. Rouen faïence often imitated Italian majolica and Dutch delftware, but gradually developed a distinct local style, marked by complex floral panels and scrolling acanthus leaves. Older pieces are typically a little heavy and have a thick, glossy glaze. Common colorways include blue on white or polychrome, paired with lobed edges and finely hand-painted decoration.

Terre de fer (northern France)

First developed in England in the early nineteenth century, ironstone (known as *terre de fer* in French) was quickly adopted by French manufactories, particularly in the north—most notably at Creil-Montereau, Saint-Amand, and Lunéville. Although originally a material classification, *terre de fer* has since become associated with a distinctly French style. Recognized for its durability, *terre de fer* produces dense, creamy-white ceramics that are often decorated with blue, green, or sepia transfer patterns. Understated floral, botanical, and pastoral motifs dominate, and originals normally bear a "Terre de fer" stamp, along with the factory name, which allows for easy identification.

Quimper (Finistère, Brittany)

Known for its *faïence populaire*, the Quimper style often depicts Breton couples in traditional dress, shown in profile, set against rustic backdrops. Other classic motifs include birds and floral garlands, in a distinctive palette of yellow, blue, green, manganese, and rust red. The most celebrated workshop is the Henriot manufactory (est. 1690), followed by HB (Hubaudière Bousquet). Many authentic nineteenth- and early twentieth-century pieces are still available on the market today, identifiable by their combination of slip-trailed outlines and freely brushed details.

Limoges (Nouvelle-Aquitaine)

The town of Limoges in the Haute-Vienne département has long been a hub of artistry. It was initially known for its faïence in the 1730s, but production transformed after the discovery of kaolin in its soil in the 1770s, enabling the production of true hard-paste porcelain. Celebrated for its translucency and refined decoration, often featuring birds, flowers, and pastoral motifs on a pure white background, Limoges porcelain quickly gained renown. Among its most devoted admirers was Marie Antoinette, who collected the pieces avidly and even commissioned designs in her own likeness. Today, Limoges remains synonymous with fine porcelain, and its creations are coveted by collectors and connoisseurs worldwide.

Apt (Provence)

The small market town of Apt is well known for its beautiful faïence d'Apt, and, in particular, for its remarkable *terres mêlées*. Plates, tureens, pitchers, and covered dishes are made either entirely in the mixed-clay finish or with a more refined design featuring a white border and crisp white handles on lids and cups.

Moustiers-Sainte-Marie (Provence)

This village in the south of France began producing faïence in the late 1680s, under the patronage of Louis XIV. Motifs like grotesques, mythological scenes, and chinoiserie are common, depicted in blue and white, manganese purple, or rich polychrome. Reproductions abound, but hallmarks from Clérissy, Ferrat, Olérys, or Fouque, as well as pinholes in the glaze and hand-painted, irregular brushstrokes, are an indication of authenticity.

Biot (Côte d'Azur)

Located in the hills behind Antibes, the town of Biot is best known for its rustic, bubble glassware and simple terra-cotta pottery: bowls, jugs, and confit pots glazed in warm hues of honey, olive green, and ocher. The town's signature technique, developed in the mid-twentieth century, suspends tiny air bubbles within the molten glass, giving each piece a soft, effervescent quality. Objects are typically handblown, with thick walls, subtle irregularities, rounded silhouettes, and jewel-toned or smoky tints. Still made in Biot today, these tactile objects are valued as much for their everyday utility as for their charm.

Vintage plates and an antique water jug from Biot in the distinctive Provençal green.

Monaco

Renowned for its art nouveau and art deco ceramics and glassware, Monaco's workshops produced tableware distinguished by gilded or luster glazes and neoclassical or vibrant Mediterranean motifs. While many ceramic pieces were left unsigned, the craftsmanship is unmistakable—double-handled jugs, exaggerated spouts and plate rims, and dense florals in bold tones of ocher, black, and turquoise. The region's glassware shares a similar decorative language; it is often etched or enameled, with geometric or floral patterns, and delicate gilding echoing the opulence of the Riviera in its heyday.

Vallauris (Côte d'Azur)

Pablo Picasso's residency at the Madoura studio in Vallauris from 1946 to 1955 elevated the town's reputation and inspired bold experimentation among local artisans. Pieces are sculptural or hefty in construction, with thick ocher, turquoise, rust, and black glazes, and lava-like surfaces. Motifs of suns, birds, or abstract reliefs are also common. Pitchers known as *demoiselles d'Avignon* are a particularly prized product from the area, recognizable by their playful silhouettes, bold palettes, and sometimes vaguely cubist or figurative forms. Hand-built or slip-cast, they usually feature asymmetrical details, stylized spouts, or rope-like handles. *Jarres à confit* (confit pots) are another typical object from the region; made in earthenware, they are often glazed on the upper half only, in yellow or olive green, and feature double handles and thick rims. Used from the eighteenth to early twentieth centuries, most surviving examples date to the late 1800s. Today, these pots are widely sought after, for use as decorative kitchen storage containers or planters.

Ciboure and Saint-Jean-de-Luz (Basque country)

Between 1910 and the 1930s, a wave of studio potters in southwestern France—most notably in Ciboure—pushed back against industrial uniformity, producing bold, handworked ceramics with a strong regional character. These pieces are unmistakable: they are typically globular in form, with earthy glazes and graphic motifs drawn from Basque culture, art deco, and early modernism (mainly birds, bulls, stylized florals, and geometric borders). Ceramics from this region are always marked with the town on the base, frequently accompanied by the artist's initials or a monogram. Highly collectible today, they prove that the avant-garde was not confined to Paris.

Majolica and barbotine (throughout France)

Inspired by Italian *maiolica*, this high-relief earthenware became a French decorative staple in the nineteenth century, notably through manufacturers like Sarreguemines, Longwy, and Saint-Clément. Molded fruit, vegetables, fish, and flowers feature extensively, finished in thick, glossy glazes. These joyful, often exuberant pieces are sometimes purely decorative, intended to be hung on walls. If you do plan to use them, just be aware that the raised surfaces can flake easily, so check for wear. For a similar feel with a little less fuss (and better suited to everyday use), look to barbotine—the French term for ceramic slip, which is used to create raised designs.

Antique dealer Laurence Vauclair is known for her exuberant table settings and her love of majolica.

Notable Manufactories

As well as identifying the material and region of origin of a piece, you should look out for the manufactory's stamp. Many manufactories left identifying marks on the underside of their creations, and some names are particularly sought after today.

Baccarat (1764–present)

Synonymous with cut crystal of the highest quality, Baccarat was established in Lorraine and has long been associated with royal commissions and diplomatic gifts. From wine glasses and decanters to monumental chandeliers, its designs are prized for their crisp facets, balanced forms, and satisfying heft. Acid-etched markings, featuring the brand name and a goblet, began in the 1930s, although earlier pieces may be unsigned.

Bernardaud (1863–present)

A standout among Limoges porcelain houses, Bernardaud has managed to preserve its classical identity while embracing bold, contemporary design. Its hard-paste porcelain is known for its exceptional clarity and fineness, ranging from gold-rimmed white services to pieces featuring painterly, abstract, or surrealist motifs. The house has produced limited editions with renowned artists and continues to straddle the line between haute tableware and collectible design objects.

Gien (1821–present)

Founded by Englishman Thomas Edme Hulm, Gien is one of the few faïence manufactories to enter the luxury market. Recognizable by its multicolor transfers, often layered over hand-painted details, and classical motifs such as Oiseaux de Paradis and Château de Chinon, its designs are formal, vibrant, and distinctly French. Early pieces, limited editions, and discontinued patterns are highly collectible, while newer releases are still popular on wedding registries. Pieces are commonly sold through specialist dealers and auction houses, but are increasingly found at mid-range antique fairs, especially in the Loire.

Longchamp (nineteenth century–present)

Based in Burgundy, Longchamp historically produced rustic, glazed faïence that embodied the everyday rhythms of rural French life. Often seen as a more provincial counterpart to Gien or Limoges, its sturdy earthenware ceramics were common in family homes and were sold at local markets. Pieces were practical and unpretentious, with thick rims and hand-applied floral motifs or bold glazes in green, ocher, and blue. After a pause in production, the brand reinvented their image in 2016 with a new line, playfully referencing their older designs with new finesse. Their pieces can now be found gracing the tables of some of France's most distinguished gastronomic addresses.

Carafes and tall wine glasses by Saint-Louis, produced in the 1900s.

Maison Pichon Uzès (1802–present)

Founded in Uzès, in southern France, and still family-run today, Pichon is celebrated for its rustic, hand-built forms and earth-toned glazes. Its most recognizable pieces feature rope- or lattice-rimmed plates, coil-built structures, figural handles, and thick-walled vessels in red clay finished with glossy or matte ochers, greens, and deep burgundies. While rooted in Provençal tradition, the brand has also begun collaborating with contemporary designers, resulting in its pieces being highly collectible.

Saint-Amand (1728–mid-twentieth century)

Saint-Amand was one of several key manufactories in the northern ceramic belt, producing both utilitarian and decorative faïence and *terre de fer* for the growing bourgeois market. The company was best known for its transfer-printed designs of delicate florals and monogrammed services with geometric banding. Though sometimes understated, these ceramics possess a quiet finesse. Pieces with provincial motifs or original presentation boxes are especially sought after, while sets for daily use can be found widely at flea markets across France.

Saint-Louis (1586–present)

The oldest glassworks in France, Saint-Louis, like Baccarat, is based in Lorraine and is often considered the latter's only true rival. It is known for both transparent and deeply saturated handblown, hand-cut crystal. Look out for colored stemware, patterned tumblers, intricate cutting, and gilded designs that marry technical finesse with theatrical flair.

FACING PAGE
The distinctive Corbeille (Basket) design by Maison Pichon has remained relevant throughout the years.

ABOVE
A collection of white and cream ceramics stands out against the pale blue finish of an armoire in L'Isle-sur-la-Sorgue.

Sarreguemines (1790s–2007)

Established during the French Revolution, Sarreguemines flourished under Napoleon and became a nineteenth-century favorite for majolica, barbotine, and fine transferware. Based in Lorraine, its pieces often feature hunting scenes, romantic landscapes, and stylized florals, and are highly prized by collectors and decorators alike. Pieces are still widely available at *brocantes* and on French auction sites, but watch out for post-World War II reproductions.

The Collector's Eye

When selecting antique tableware, you should consider not only its aesthetic and historical significance but also its suitability for use today. For everyday purposes, you might look for durable materials such as stoneware, which can easily withstand frequent handling. However, don't imagine you have to save delicate patterned china for special occasions only. Aim to create a collection that seamlessly blends durability with elegance, enhancing daily rituals as well as celebrations.

Once you've found a piece that meets your needs, it's time to inspect the markings. For faïence, the *Dictionnaire des Marques de Faïence* lists over six thousand traditional makers' marks—helpfully, it can be accessed online. Porcelain typically carries a manufactory backstamp, which can also be cross-checked in specialist guides. True crystal often features etched or acid-stamped signatures, but not always; for example, postwar Baccarat introduced a circular logo marked "Baccarat France," but earlier pieces may be unsigned or simply bear a paper label. Be sure to ask for documentation wherever possible.

While it certainly pays to familiarize yourself with period-specific details, try not to get caught up in rarity alone. Choose pieces you love, that complement your personal style and home, and don't be afraid to mix and match. Layering different styles—Quimper plates with Biot bowls, for instance—creates character.

Some imperfection and patina should be embraced, up to a point. Always check for hairline cracks, chips, pitting, faded gilding, and signs of repair. Crazing is common in faïence and is not inherently a problem, often helping to confirm age, but deep cracks, especially near food-contact areas, are best avoided if you plan to use the piece, as they can harbor bacteria, leach lead, or weaken structural integrity. If you do encounter damaged items, be wary of over-restoration. Filled chips and reglazing may reduce value, as honest wear is often preferred by collectors over touch-ups.

Delft and Rouen plates are artfully displayed side by side at the Chatou antique fair.

Caring for Antique Tableware

Keep your antique tableware within easy reach, so it never feels like a hassle to use. When stacking, slip a napkin or sheet of paper towel between each plate to prevent scratches, and when removing a dish, always lift rather than slide, to avoid grazing the glaze.

Long periods in storage are not ideal since fluctuating humidity can weaken glazes and lead to hairline cracks. If you're not using your china regularly, take it out at least once a year, give it a gentle wash, and let it air out. This keeps the surface strong and the glaze intact.

The temptation is to wash all tableware in the dishwasher, and for late nineteenth-century and twentieth-century services this can be fine. Glazed pieces (you'll know by the smooth, glossy finish) can usually go in the dishwasher on a gentle cycle—just don't overcrowd the racks. Leave enough space so pieces don't knock against each other.

Older services are often larger than today's standard dimensions, and might not fit easily into a modern dishwasher—these should be hand-washed, along with unglazed or gilded items. Nineteenth-century transferware is also best washed by hand, as humidity can get beneath the glaze and cause dark stains that are hard to remove.

Before washing, line the sink with a rubber mat or a folded dish towel to prevent chipping, and clean with a mild detergent and warm water. Avoid products containing bleach, which can cause yellowing. Let pieces air-dry or pat gently with a dish towel.

Antique glassware is surprisingly resilient, but it still needs a gentle touch. Dishwashers are best avoided as the high heat and detergents can dull or crack antique crystal. When washing by hand, line the sink with a rubber mat or use a plastic basin to avoid any breakages. Otherwise, warm soapy water, a soft cloth, a good rinse, and a careful dry are all it takes.

For vintage crystal decanters or carafes, avoid storing spirits or wine long-term, as lead may leach into the liquid. If buildup from the liquid occurs, fill with warm water and a splash of vinegar or a denture-cleaning tablet. Let the mixture sit for an hour, then rinse and dry straight away using a lint-free cloth to prevent water marks.

With a little attention, your tableware will serve for another century—and look just as beautiful as the day it was made.

FACING PAGE
Pink-and-white plates by de Havilland, featuring the Arbre de Vie (Tree of Life) design.

PAGE 88
Asparagus plates from Salins dating from 1900.

PAGE 89
A complete set of Limoges tableware displayed by specialist Eva Cwajg at the Puces de Saint-Ouen.

PAGES 90–91
White shell-shaped *raviers*—shallow dishes for serving appetizers—in Limoges porcelain.

MEET THE EXPERT

Eva Cwajg

Les Tables d'Eva
Marché Serpette, Puces de Saint-Ouen
lestablesdeva.fr
@lestablesdeva

For Eva Cwajg, the Puces de Saint-Ouen, to the north of Paris, is her second home. Her father sold antiques here, as did her grandfather. Although she initially resisted, Eva eventually opened her own boutiques in the labyrinth of dealers—first in the Marché Vernaison, and now in the Marché Serpette.

A mecca for antique tableware aficionados, particularly those seeking porcelain and china services, this is not the place to come for a single plate to mix into your everyday set. Eva is one of the few dealers who focus on complete antique services, often comprising one hundred to two hundred pieces—all in immaculate condition.

Like many in the trade, Eva's specialty reflects her personal taste. She has a passion for tablescapes, and her two shops always feature beautifully styled arrangements of her latest finds. While she primarily deals in French porcelain, she occasionally includes Italian, German, or Swedish sets, and her preferred period is 1880 to 1940. She mainly sources her wares from early morning antique fairs, and occasionally from auction houses, if the right sale is on.

Clients come—and return—to Eva's stores because they love her taste. She sometimes receives orders from long-term customers, but most often people come to be inspired. Her clientele is partly French, but largely international, especially American. With her vast knowledge and keen eye for detail, Eva can tell you the pedigree of any plate or tureen in her collection, and just as readily suggest the perfect flatware or glassware to go with it.

EVA'S TIPS

Whenever possible, buy in person. You'll get a better sense of weight, texture, and glaze quality, and you'll be able to spot any tiny flaws. Shopping in regional ceramic hubs improves your chances of finding authentic antiques and locally made items; village *brocantes* and château clearances often yield the most interesting finds.

CHAPTER 5

Rugs and Tapestries

Tapestries are a specialized sector, with a specific clientele. Originally hung as wall coverings in lieu of frescoes, tapestries were made for large rooms in châteaux, or edifices with high ceilings and long walls, such as state buildings or churches. Woven in rich shades from natural dyes, these monumental works once draped entire rooms, their dense wool and silk trapping heat as much as drawing attention. Today, a full-scale tapestry can be hard to place in a contemporary home—its size is simply overpowering. Yet despite their challenging scale, tapestries are making a quiet comeback. Fragments—salvaged and reimagined—often find new life as ottoman or cushion covers, used as striking wall panels, or even as room dividers.

Antique rugs are more versatile, with the advantage of coming in all sizes. Passed down through generations, they've become timeless elements in home décor, and it's relatively easy to find one that suits a modern space and is still in good condition. A rug that is tired, perhaps a little ragged around the edges, can still be shown with pride—and if the patina has gone too far, in most cases, it can be repaired.

An eighteenth-century Aubusson tapestry in wool and silk depicting a château, with a bird and flowers in the foreground.

Rug Manufactories

France's long-held love of rugs began in the sixteenth century, when an alliance with the Ottoman Empire ushered a steady stream of Turkish and Persian carpets into aristocratic interiors. These were more than decorative—they were cultural capital, signaling political ties, refined taste, and elite status. By the early seventeenth century, admiration had turned to emulation. Keen to restore French craftsmanship, Henry IV established several workshops to produce carpets in the oriental style for his palaces. From this emerged two defining traditions: Savonnerie and Aubusson.

Savonnerie

Founded in a former soap factory on the Seine (*savon* is the French word for soap, hence the name), the Savonnerie manufactory was state-sponsored and had clear goals: to revive French luxury production, rival Persian artistry, and establish a national style. Early Savonnerie carpets imitated Ottoman motifs, but a unique French aesthetic quickly took hold. Helmed by Charles Le Brun, a famous artist, architect, and official painter at the court of Louis XIV until the late 1600s, the manufactory introduced a baroque sensibility that would set the tone for French rugs for decades. Instead of arabesques and intricate foliage patterns, Savonnerie style was characterized by cartouche designs, acanthus scrolls, and multiple borders. At its peak, Savonnerie's output was reserved for royal and ecclesiastical commissions, earning these richly ornamented carpets a reputation as the Versailles of rugs.

Aubusson

While Savonnerie dealt in thick, knotted-pile rugs, Aubusson, located in central France, specialized in flat-woven pieces using tapestry looms. These *tapis ras* (low-pile carpets) were lighter in both hand and style, favoring neoclassical medallions, garlands, and florals in faded pastels. By the eighteenth century, as rococo replaced baroque, Aubusson's aesthetic was further finessed. Designer Pierre-Josse Perrot introduced the kind of detailing we now associate with French refinement: wreaths, ribbons, and trailing garland motifs—ornate and unapologetically decorative.

Beauvais

Aubusson's rise coincided with that of Beauvais, another center for tapestry and carpet production. Both towns thrived in the 1800s, and Beauvais developed its own soft and ornate visual language. Its romantic bow motifs and trailing botanicals—rendered with elegant restraint—came to define the look of French interiors, especially as faster looms and modern techniques brought these pieces beyond the elite and into private homes.

This Persian rug, hung as a tapestry, portrays the Garden of Eden with all of its flora and fauna.

Tapestry Manufactories

France's tapestry tradition runs even deeper than its rug production. By the 1400s, workshops in Arras and Paris were already weaving intricate backgrounds of millefleurs (dense scatterings of individual flowers), along with mythic beasts and courtly allegories. The most famous example, *The Lady and the Unicorn*, now hangs in the Musée de Cluny in Paris. These early tapestries weren't just decorative—they were symbolic, instructive, political, and devotional. The making of these tapestries was a collaborative effort. It started with an artist's sketch of the initial design. A cartoonist then translated it into a full-scale panel—works of art in their own right, they are sometimes found at antiques fairs, rolled up like wallpaper scrolls. Next, colorists selected the exact shades of wool or silk, and finally, weavers, often working for months or even years, slowly brought the image to life.

Over time, tapestry shifted from religious storytelling to royal propaganda, from architectural grandeur to decorative intimacy, and finally to modern reinvention. At its height under Louis XIV, it was a tool of soft power and statecraft. But by the late eighteenth century, that grandeur had begun to unravel. The French Revolution gutted demand. Many tapestries were burned for their metallic threads; others simply fell out of favor. A brief Napoleonic revival embraced neoclassical themes, but the golden age had passed. By the nineteenth century, tapestries had become scaled-down copies of their regal ancestors, their motifs smaller and messages lighter.

ABOVE, LEFT AND FACING PAGE
The famous cartoons of Aubusson allowed tapestry weavers to create works true to the original artist's design. Today, they can be framed as works of art in their own right.

ABOVE, RIGHT
A detail from an eighteenth-century tapestry depicting *feuillage*, or foliage.

In the twentieth century, however, tapestry was revivified. Artists like Jean Lurçat, working in Aubusson, reimagined it as a modern medium—bold, graphic, and politically charged once more. His work reignited interest, leading to new commissions and a rethinking of tapestry as art rather than ornament. For those collecting or styling antique tapestries, the three main manufactories below are worth noting.

Gobelins

Originally a private workshop known for its dyeing expertise, Gobelins was transformed into a royal manufactory in 1662, directed by Charles Le Brun. The Gobelins tapestries became the visual expression of Louis XIV's court: high baroque and dramatic in style, and almost propagandistic in tone. Subjects were chosen as carefully as color: military campaigns, classical mythology, and biblical epics. Featuring gold-threaded borders and deep chiaroscuro, they were designed to travel, to impress, and to endure. Typically produced in editions of no more than six, their rarity only heightens their value today.

Beauvais

Unlike Gobelins, Beauvais was never a royal manufactory. Its focus was domestic, specializing in chair covers, fire screens, and panel inserts—smaller works embellished with garlands, ribbons, and chinoiserie. In the eighteenth century, as with rugs, tapestry design became less grand, with the rococo style ushering in garden fantasies and flirtatious motifs. These pieces brought tapestry into private interiors, turning a grand art into a more intimate one.

Aubusson

Also known for its rugs, Aubusson produced flat-woven tapestries and needlepoint-style panels that shared the same painterly touch and light-handed motifs. Unlike the fine, precise hatching of Gobelins stitching, Aubusson's thicker weave gave the work a more rustic, textured feel.

By the eighteenth century, under designers such as Pierre-Josse Perrot, Aubusson had developed a signature look: pale greens, shell pinks, and dusty blues woven into garlands, urns, latticework, and pastoral scenes.

La Sirène (The Mermaid), designed by Jean Picart Le Doux and woven by Aubusson in 1970.

The Collector's Eye

French rugs and tapestries are as versatile as they are beautiful. While their patterns and patina feel right at home in traditional French interiors, they're equally compelling placed in modern homes, paired with relaxed textures, or amid bohemian décors.

When you find a tapestry at a *brocante* or flea market, the first thing to look at is whether the design is truly woven or simply printed on fabric. A genuine tapestry is entirely made from interwoven threads, which gives it texture and depth.

While age and wear give antique rugs and tapestries their character, there's a difference between charmingly weathered and structurally unsound. If you can, view them flat on the floor—not hung—and in natural light, examining both back and front. This reveals loose threads, warping, bulges, or other irregularities that may not be visible at eye level.

Run your hand along the back to spot repairs, and check the edges for fraying, missing borders, or broken warp—structural threads that run vertically down the textile, which can weaken over time. A high-quality rug or tapestry will have a tight, even weave and consistent tension, and the ends and selvedges should feel secure.

You'll also want to look out for signs of redyeing. Many antique French rugs were colored with natural vegetable dyes, which soften beautifully over time to create the gentle tonal variations known as "abrash." Synthetic dyes, by contrast, can appear overly bright, signaling heavy-handed restoration or later alterations.

Alongside condition, it's equally important to understand the material. Older or high-quality tapestries are often made from wool, sometimes silk,

ABOVE, LEFT
A detail from *Le Coq et les Astres* (The Rooster and the Stars), designed by Jean Lurçat and woven by Aubusson in 1950–1960.

ABOVE, RIGHT
Écume (Sea Foam), designed by Jean Picart Le Doux and woven from wool and cotton by Aubusson in the 1950s.

ABOVE, LEFT AND RIGHT
Tapestries are meticulously repaired and restored before being dispatched to clients—a task that requires expert knowledge and a lot of patience.

and these materials can be recognized by touch and sight: wool is dense and supple, silk is shinier. While wool rugs are wonderfully forgiving, silk is more fragile, and cotton falls somewhere in between. When choosing the material of a rug, think practically: Where will it be placed? Is it in danger of spills, or heavy footfall? A rug you love is a joy—but it also needs to suit the rhythm of your home.

For tapestries, consider both their subject and scale. Antique examples can be immense, originally made for grand, formal rooms. While it's tempting to fall for a large, dramatic panel, think realistically about your wall space. Smaller pieces or fragments can be just as powerful and easier to display.

To estimate a tapestry's age and origin, observe the style of the design, the materials used, the weaving technique, and any marks or signatures. Quality always shows in the details. The finer and more precise the design, the more time and care it likely took to make. The subject and colors can also offer clues. A well-composed scene—with figures, landscapes, or classical décor—may indicate that it came from a well-known workshop.

Rugs and tapestries often pass through many hands before they reach your own, so provenance matters. When possible, ask where and when the piece was made, and whether it has undergone any repairs—honest dealers will be transparent about age, condition, and restoration. In case of doubt, consult an expert who can provide a precise assessment of its origin.

Practicalities aside, the real test is emotional. The most powerful pieces don't just fill the space—they transform it. This is especially true for tapestries, which are more than decorative—they're narrative works. Whether it's a pastoral or mythological scene, choose one that draws you in; it will set the tone for the whole room.

Caring for Rugs and Tapestries

Antique rugs and tapestries respond best to a gentle hand and regular care. Left uncleaned, dirt and dust can dull their luster and shorten their lifespan significantly. You'll need to know the material make-up of your rug or tapestry to care for it properly. Though often more resilient than they appear, some weaves and materials are better suited to quieter corners of the home. Silk rugs, while exquisite, are especially sensitive and best kept out of high-traffic areas. Thicker piles can handle more foot traffic, while finer, flatter rugs are best reserved for bedrooms or lower-use spaces. Both silk and cotton stain more easily than wool, and all natural fibers can quickly degrade if exposed to sunlight for too long, causing dyes to fade and fibers to weaken. If your rug or tapestry catches the sun during the day, you may want to consider installing sheer curtains to help diffuse the light. One simple but effective habit for increasing longevity: take off your shoes indoors. Your rug will thank you.

Most of us walk the same paths through our homes each day, so rotating rugs is essential to avoid uneven wear. A simple 180-degree turn every six months helps preserve a uniform appearance. Particularly delicate rugs—or those more than three hundred years old—are often best displayed as wall hangings, where they can be admired without risk.

If your rug tends to slip, a high-quality underlay is a worthwhile investment. It improves safety, protects the weave, and adds a layer of comfort underfoot. Just be sure to choose one that won't leave residue on textiles or flooring. In some cases, you might want to consider adding a canvas backing to your rug, which can increase its durability.

ABOVE, LEFT
A fragment of a sixteenth-century tapestry from Brussels is draped across the arm of a seventeenth-century upholstered armchair.

ABOVE, RIGHT
A detail from an Aubusson tapestry dating from 1850.

ABOVE, LEFT
Tapestries available to purchase are carefully rolled and labelled, making it easy to identify each piece at a glance, before unrolling it for a closer inspection.

ABOVE, RIGHT
In Max Jabert's store, a fragment of an eighteenth-century tapestry adorns the back of a chair.

PAGE 104
A sixteenth-century Feuille de Choux tapestry by Atelier de la Marche.

PAGE 105
Carefully folded remnants of larger tapestries.

PAGES 106–107
Beautiful rolls of Aubusson tapestry cartoons, ready to be framed.

Old tapestries should also be lined to prevent the weaving threads on the back from separating. A lining can protect the tapestry from dust and climate variations, but if poorly applied or too tight, it can create tension and damage the piece, so it's best left to a professional.

Every type of rug—modern or antique—benefits from a weekly vacuum. For delicate pieces, avoid rotary brushes, which can be too aggressive. Go lightly, vacuuming in all directions, and taking care around the borders. Every so often, flip over the rug to vacuum the back. For very fragile rugs, a soft outdoor shake (or a gentle cleaning with a cane rug beater) can work wonders.

Spills are best tackled fast. Instead of hot water or carpet steamers—which can lead to warping, shrinking, or fading—gentle methods work best. Start by vacuuming or shaking out any loose debris. Dab a mild solution of carpet detergent, white vinegar, and warm water sparingly onto the stain or spill. Using a soft-bristled brush, gently work the solution into the pile using small, cautious strokes, being careful not to scrub. Gently pat dry and leave flat in a well-ventilated space.

Moths can wreak havoc on vintage textiles, so regular inspection is key. An annual professional cleaning is a smart precaution, and if you're planning on putting your textiles into storage, ensure they're completely dry—dampness is an open invitation to pests—and stored in a protective cover made from clean, white cotton cloth, or from muslin.

If you're unsure how to handle a fragile or particularly valuable rug or tapestry, ask for help. Professional cleaners who specialize in antique textiles have the right tools and knowledge to treat them with the respect they deserve, restoring their beauty without risk.

MEET THE EXPERT

Max Jabert

Galerie Jabert
Village Suisse, Paris
galeriejabert.com
@galerie_jabert

MAX'S TIPS

If a tapestry is very damaged or full of holes, it can still be given a second life as cushions or upholstery. Start by identifying the best-preserved sections: readable motifs, stable weaving, and unfaded colors. These can be carefully cut out and reused.

Before any transformation, reinforce the tapestry with a backing fabric to stabilize it and prevent additional tearing. Avoid areas that are too worn—they won't hold up over time.

For a polished, lasting result, it's best to work with a professional upholsterer or textile artisan. They'll know how to highlight the robust parts while respecting the fabric's fragility. And when using antique tapestry on furniture, protect it: reduce friction, avoid direct light, and use it decoratively rather than functionally.

Max Jabert, a third-generation dealer, comes from a family of Persian descent. His ancestors left Iran for Germany, and during World War II fled again, seeking refuge in France.

Specializing in tapestries from the 1500s to the 2000s, Max only buys what he truly loves. "A tapestry has to speak to me," he says, "before I even ask about its condition or the price." Many of the pieces in his catalog come from châteaux around France and, occasionally, Belgium.

Before resale, every tapestry is cleaned with care and attention, using nonchemical products, then passed to a specialist for any essential repairs. Colors are never retouched. "It's rarely necessary," Max explains. "The original dyes—like indigo, curcuma, and madder—don't fade with sunlight, or even moonlight."

Each piece is appraised, gently restored, and often lined with soft cotton for support, then carefully rolled and stored in his Paris boutique at the Village Suisse. Just steps from the Eiffel Tower, this quiet enclave is home to a close-knit group of experts in paintings, jewelry, furniture—and, of course, tapestries and rugs. There is a friendly atmosphere between the dealers, who are open every day except Tuesdays and Wednesdays.

CHAPTER 6

Textiles and Home Linens

It's easy to collect linens until your cupboards are full to overflowing, not least because they are so useful. Curtains give warmth and texture to a room; tablecloths and napkins add charm to table settings; and the quality of bed linens can make the difference between a good or bad night's sleep. Nineteenth-century linen bed sheets, for example, provide incomparable comfort: warm in the winter, cool in the summer, these amazing threads of flax, spun and woven more than a century ago, still have their place in the modern home.

There is also the pleasure—and here I speak from personal experience—of opening an armoire and seeing piles of beautifully pressed tablecloths, sheets, pillow shams, and more. Before you know it, you'll have accumulated more linens than you can use in a lifetime, and you'll start smuggling any new purchases into the home when nobody is around to see.

In the antiques world there are many dealers who specialize in textiles. The purists, who disregard anything later than eighteenth-century items, offer intricate floral textiles and faded linens with motifs that are still being replicated today. Those looking for sturdier items can easily find table linens in today's markets. From long tablecloths to individually embroidered napkins, which were traditionally part of a young bride's trousseau, these linens are hard-wearing and can be used daily.

Eighteenth-century toiles, dyed in indigo and folded, in front of a painted screen from the same period.

The Trousseau

From the fourteenth century to the early twentieth century, the tradition of preparing the bride's trousseau was widely respected in France. Brides at the time were expected to arrive in their new homes equipped with a wide array of household linens and personal accessories, from kitchen towels to nightgowns. When a daughter was born, her mother and grandmother would begin organizing the creation of these items for her trousseau, all home spun, sewn, and embroidered.

Assembling a beautiful collection of linens for the young bride was a matter of great pride, and a sign of family wealth. Families of considerable means may have reserved the production of linen from an entire field of flax for their daughter's needs, thus ensuring a consistent quality and feel to the fabric. Affluent families often employed a seamstress responsible for all the household linen requirements, including the trousseau. In families without their own seamstress, however, the task of creating and embroidering fell to the future bride and her female relatives. For the young woman's wardrobe, they confected dresses, blouses, and skirts, petticoats, underclothes, and aprons, and headdresses and bonnets, while for her home the list of essentials included sheets, pillowcases, tablecloths, towels, kitchen towels, and handkerchiefs. Typically, the bride would have been provided with twelve of each, but in well-to-do families, it was not unheard of to supply a round hundred. Public trousseau viewings were held in the weeks leading up to a wedding, designed to impress the community with the quality of the bride's linens.

Today, we continue to enjoy the fruit of this tradition. Once unthinkable, we happily use monogrammed linens with initials that don't match our own, simply for the beauty and quality of the needlework. You might come across these tablecloths and napkins dyed in rich modern hues, with the monogram taking on a deeper tone than the rest of the fabric.

FACING PAGE
Delicately embroidered and beribboned nightshirts—apparently unused—with the ink of the monogram design still clearly visible.

ABOVE
During the late nineteenth and early twentieth centuries, monogrammed bedsheets were the pride and joy of new brides.

Hand-Stitched Details

Until the end of the nineteenth century, all home linens were hand stitched, with seams, hems, embroidery, lace, and monograms all painstakingly created by the homemaker or her seamstress. Occasionally, in addition to the hems and monogram, sheets may have a central hand-stitched seam running down the length of the fabric—when the full width of the sheet couldn't be accommodated on a regular loom, the sheet was woven in two sections and hand stitched together. If it was to be monogrammed, the letters would then be carefully embroidered on either side of the seam. Every so often, I come across bedding with initials on the outer corners of the sheet instead of in the center. For a long time I couldn't figure out why this would be, until I noticed the fabric's extensive wear. Back in the day, when the sheet began to show signs of thinning in the center, the seamstress would patiently undo the central seam, and switch the panels so that the thinner fabric was now on the outer edges, effectively extending the sheet's lifespan.

ABOVE
At her store in Provence, Nathalie Massett dyes antique linens by hand to achieve her own color palette.

FACING PAGE
A pile of nineteenth-century nightshirts emerge from an armoire, displaying the embroidered monograms of their original owner.

M.D
M.D

Regional Specialties

France's textile heritage comprises a wealth of regional techniques and styles. Here are some of the most renowned.

Boutis and courtepointe

These hand-stitched quilts were assembled from two layers of fabric, stuffed with wadding to create a raised pattern. They are a specialty from the south of France, typically made in Marseille and the region of Provence. Often featuring floral patterns and pastoral scenes, these quilts were typically part of the bridal trousseau or given as baptismal blankets, and today are prized for their intricacy and durability. Traditionally the term *boutis* is used for covers made solely with white fabric, while *courtepointe* or *couvertures piqués* are made with richly colored fabrics.

Dentelle

French lace or dentelle, widely used to embellish clothing and household lines, was produced in several different northern hubs. In Normandy, Alençon was known for its fine-needle lace with elaborate floral patterns, while Chantilly, to the northeast of Paris, was famous for its delicate black bobbin lace with a fine mesh background. Valenciennes, near the Belgian border, produced softer, net-like lace often used in trims.

ABOVE, LEFT
An assortment of lace and embroidered organza on offer at the Villeneuve-lès-Avignon fair.

ABOVE, RIGHT
A Chinese fabric, indigo dyed and embroidered, originally used for carrying a baby.

FACING PAGE
Hand-quilted eighteenth-century bed covers, displayed in a hand-painted wooden chest.

Harvest supper tablecloths

Typically made from heavy linen or *métis* (a blend of linen and cotton), reflecting rural French traditions, these oversized, sturdy tablecloths from Burgundy and Bordeaux were decorated simply. Featuring natural motifs, stripes, or monograms, they were used to cover the long tables at communal feasts celebrating the end of the harvest. Passed down through the generations, they became cherished heirlooms; today, you'll often see them seamlessly integrated into modern shabby-chic table settings.

Toile de Jouy

Produced in Jouy-en-Josas, near Paris, in the eighteenth century, this printed cotton became famous for depicting pastoral scenes and neoclassical motifs. Traditionally, the design was monochromatic, most often in blue, pink, red, green, or black. Appreciated for its whimsical narratives, toile de Jouy was a popular choice for bed linens, wall coverings, curtains, and other forms of upholstery well into the nineteenth century.

ABOVE
Antique ironstone plates from Moustiers arranged on a striking red-and-white linen tablecloth.

FACING PAGE
Remnants of distinctive eighteenth- and nineteenth-century fabrics.

Chafarcanis and indiennes

Introduced to France from the Ottoman Empire and India in the seventeenth century, these block-printed and hand-painted cotton fabrics gained immense popularity in Provence and Alsace, and were used for curtains, bedspreads, table linens, and clothing. Indiennes featured elaborate florals and exotic patterns, whereas *chafarcanis* were simpler, with small geometric or floral motifs in shades of red and white. While *chafarcanis* are regionally specific, indiennes had wider appeal. These printed textiles were so in demand that local artisans began replicating them, despite a royal ban in 1686 on the sale, production, and even the wearing of printed fabric in order to protect domestic (royal) industries. One of the most famous brands, Souleiado, has been printing traditional indiennes and other Provençal iterations since the sixteenth century, preserving this rich heritage. To this day, these textiles remain a symbol of French craftsmanship and a staple of Provençal décor.

Kelsch

This traditional fabric from Alsace is woven from linen and either wool or cotton. Recognizable by its signature checks or stripes in shades of red, blue, and white, it has been handcrafted for centuries using natural dyes and time-honored weaving techniques. Originally made for household linens, curtains, and clothing, *kelsch* fabric embodies Alsatian heritage and craftsmanship. It remains a cherished textile, valued for its durability and rustic charm.

FACING PAGE
On a garden ladder hang various indiennes—designs associated with Provence.

ABOVE, LEFT AND RIGHT
Traditional nineteenth-century Provençal costume, comprising a caraco and a gathered skirt.

FACING PAGE
Folded linens and *courtepointes* on a simple wooden stool.

ABOVE, LEFT AND RIGHT
Textiles are not only about pretty fabrics; here, umbrellas and a simple drape bear witness to the passing years.

PAGES 122 AND 123
Red dyes made from the madder plant were typically used in Provence to tint fabrics and create indienne prints.

The Collector's Eye

Thoroughly examine the condition of antique linens. Unfold napkins to check for stains or loose threads and look out for holes or thin patches on sheets. Small tears can be mended, but real wear and tear on a sheet makes it unusable, however appealing the design.

When buying quilts, pay attention to the stuffing. Good quilts should feel smooth and supple, and consistently padded. Lumpy, uneven filling often means it has been poorly stored and the wadding has started to degrade. Not only will a lumpy quilt look messy on a bed, it will provide uneven warmth and will wear faster.

Patina—the hallmark of the natural aging process of an item—is not a quality reserved solely for artwork and furniture. Over time, fabric fades and grows softer. Linens may discolor slightly and begin to fray due to exposure to light, frequent use, and contact with the oils from our skin. This ageing process adds character and depth to textiles and can even make them more desirable to collectors—unique markings are a sign of authenticity and can reveal a piece's history.

When buying antique linens, look for a balanced patina: enough to suggest age and use, but not so much that it compromises the fabric's integrity or usability. Wear should feel natural: soft fading along folds; changes in color or texture of the embroidery; expert repairs that enhance the overall aesthetic of the piece. Avoid sheets that feel overly stiff or rough—these may have been cleaned or stored improperly—and instead prioritize softness, the sign of a well-worn but well-cared-for item.

MEET THE EXPERT

Monique Alphand

Private collection, Provence

Monique Alphand, a former Greek and Latin teacher, has dedicated herself to reviving the appreciation of *chafarcani* and other French textiles. Her passion for collecting began in 1973 when she discovered a box of vintage fabrics at a *brocante*. Drawn in by their beauty, she soon became intrigued by their history, and has since spent decades carefully hunting down and studying textiles from across France. Now an authority on the subject, she has amassed a collection that is nothing short of remarkable, transforming her home into a living textile museum.

The collection spans Provençal quilts, antique costumes, and a wealth of *chafarcani* pieces, many of whose origins Monique can trace through stamped marks—a practice introduced in 1759. These stamps provide insight into where and by whom the textiles were produced, revealing how high demand in the eighteenth century led to faster, less refined manufacturing methods.

Today, Monique's collection remains private, but she shares her knowledge and sometimes sells select pieces to those who appreciate their historical value. Her dedication keeps *chafarcani* from being forgotten, preserving its place in history for future generations.

MONIQUE'S TIPS

While fine fabrics are a wonderful addition to a collection, fragments, offcuts, and pieces with simple motifs are also desirable and are well worth collecting. Even the most worn and faded pieces retain a quiet dignity—a reminder of the fabric's enduring charm and modest sophistication.

Caring for Textiles

Long gone are the days when linens were carried down to the village washhouse on the river, where maids knelt on the ground, exchanging gossip as they scrubbed the fabric in the flowing water. Back then, the huge sheets and tablecloths were spread out to dry on meadow grass. As the chloroform in the grass reacted to the sunshine, it released oxygen, bleaching the fabric and maintaining its whiteness.

Thankfully, nineteenth-century bed linens are surprisingly robust, and today they can be washed in modern washing machines. These fabrics benefit from a hot wash, which helps to break down stains and maintain brightness naturally. Since tumble drying can weaken linen fibers, line dry when possible. In the case of stubborn stains, apply lemon juice and leave the fabric to dry in the sunshine. If the stain persists, a chemical stain-remover may be effective.

Older fabrics, in particular *boutis* or *courtepointe*, can be gently hand-washed and dried outside, or entrusted to an expert dry cleaner who understands how to treat these more fragile textiles. Wool can become hard if improperly stored, so make sure not to fold your quilts too tightly. Store them flat or loose in a breathable fabric bag, away from light and moisture, when not in use.

When storing antique linens, it is best to press and fold them neatly and keep them behind closed doors. Exposure to light for long periods can cause white fabric to take on a yellowish hue, which is surprisingly difficult to remove. Colored fabrics can fade if left exposed to sun or moonlight.

An armoire is perfect for storing linens, and can look equally attractive on a landing, in a laundry room, or in a guest bedroom. Store your linens flat on the shelves, in beautifully ordered rows, by type or by color. Before storing, line the shelves or drawers with acid-free tissue paper to prevent your linens from degrading or staining. You can also wrap your finer linens in a clean, undyed sheet as a reusable alternative—just make sure to wash it regularly.

ABOVE
An iron daybed dressed with a mix of antique *chafarcani*.

FACING PAGE
Antique fabrics should always be hand-washed and left to air-dry.

PAGE 126
An artful display at Atelier des Textiles Anciens.

PAGE 127
A mid-eighteenth-century cupboard with a hand-painted interior is suspended over a chest of drawers brimming with seventeenth- and eighteenth-century fabrics.

PAGES 128–129
An eighteenth-century bed is the perfect setting for an eclectic collection of Provençal garments, religious robes, and cashmere shawls.

MEET THE EXPERT

Jérôme Prévost

Atelier des Textiles Anciens
Tarascon, Provence
@atelier_textiles_anciens

Jérôme's affinity with textiles seemingly comes naturally, woven into the very fabric of his family history. Growing up around his grandmother, who was a seamstress, and his Italian grandfather, a tailor, he has vivid memories of life in the atelier, filled with bolts of fabric, pincushions, and the rhythmic sound of scissors slicing through cloth.

In addition to his family ties, Jérôme was born in Lille, the historic heart of France's textile industry, where he absorbed the traditions of his region. He later moved to Paris to study fashion, specializing in textile creation. It was during this time that fate played its hand. A close friend—an antique silverware dealer—introduced him to the world of *brocantes* and antique fairs. While accompanying him, Jérôme found himself irresistibly drawn to antique textiles. He began collecting white monogrammed linens, then *boutis* and quilted blankets; each piece had a story just waiting to be uncovered. Since then, he has been on a continual quest for the next remarkable fabric.

A defining moment of his career came when he purchased a stunning bed cover, unaware of its significance. Later, while flipping through an Italian book on *tessuti*, he recognized its pattern and realized he had stumbled upon a rare piece of toile de Jouy. Stamped with an Oberkampf hallmark and sporting an "Homage de l'Amérique à la France" design, he believes the fabric dated from 1783. The piece was later sold to an American collector. This discovery cemented Jérôme's passion, setting him on a journey to seek out the experts—at the Puces de Saint-Ouen flea market near Paris and at fairs across France.

After launching his first stand at the prestigious Salon de la Bastille, Jérôme's work quickly gained a following among decorators, antique dealers, and set designers. Today, he is known for his exquisite collection of eighteenth- and nineteenth-century textiles, specializing in Provençal clothing, printed fabrics, and indiennes.

Jérôme can be found at the Villeneuve-lès-Avignon Saturday fair, or by appointment at his showroom in Tarascon.

JÉRÔME'S TIPS

Every fabric has a past, so don't hesitate to ask a dealer about its history—it is what brings each piece to life. For Jérôme, the joy of his work lies not just in tracking down fabrics, but also in the conversations that they spark. He delights in sharing his knowledge and passion, whether clients buy or simply pause to admire.

CHAPTER 7

Jewelry

When it comes to antiquing, jewelry is perhaps the most personal choice you can make. In addition to its history, the design, colors, and feel of the piece in your hands all come into play. Whether intended for yourself or for someone special, jewelry is designed to be worn, and is a purchase to be considered carefully.

For some people, the appeal will lie in the quality of the stones, but for others, it's about the feeling or memories these pieces evoke—perhaps of a person or an event. I have very clear recollections of my great-grandmother opening up her old wooden box full of costume jewelry and asking me to choose a piece as a gift. Her name was Louise, and she had lived an exciting life, including a decade as the young wife of my great-grandfather, a soldier under the Raj in colonial India. As she opened the lid, I felt like I was discovering buried treasure. With hindsight, I know there was nothing of value in the box, but the little girl that I was at the time picked out the biggest, brightest brooch and believed it was a jewel fit for a maharaja. In reality, it was made of ordinary red glass set in a simple metal mount, but I loved it instantly and occasionally still wear it in her memory.

Today, it's relatively easy to find nineteenth-century jewelry (*bijoux*, in French); pieces from the eighteenth century or earlier, however, are rarer. This can be explained by two major upheavals: during the French Revolution, much jewelry was confiscated and broken up or melted down, while the Industrial Revolution changed manufacturing methods, making jewelry more accessible to a broader public.

Antique jewelry carries a layered history. It may be timeworn or have been damaged or altered. Stones can be loose, settings may need tightening, and metals may tarnish. But with expert care, these pieces can be restored, their stones replaced, settings secured, and surfaces tenderly polished.

Ultimately, it's a matter of following your heart. The beauty of antique jewelry is that even though jewelry design evolves, the pieces themselves do not go out of fashion. Antique jewelry spans a wide range of tastes and styles, and the finest pieces—those with rare stones, unusual settings, and refined techniques, such as eighteenth-century filigree—are often irreplaceable and impossible to reproduce.

Nineteenth-century cameo brooches and bracelets sit alongside strings of pearls, a ruby ring, and a gold Victorian necklace.

Jewelry Design Periods

For much of French history, jewelry was more about lineage, etiquette, and wealth than adornment. Until the nineteenth century, most people in rural France would never have owned a single piece of fine jewelry—a silver ring at most, or perhaps a small brass cross or religious medallion, brought back from a pilgrimage and pinned to a bodice. Gold was far beyond the reach of the average person, and during the French Revolution, even possessing gold coins was a dangerous act—one that could, for a time, carry the death penalty. Jewelry had been too closely tied to the ancien régime and the monarchy; its return to acceptability would be gradual and symbolic.

Prerevolution courtly jewelry (seventeenth and eighteenth centuries)

At the royal court, particularly under Louis XIV and Louis XV, jewelry was part and parcel of the spectacle of monarchy—an assertion of hierarchy, wealth, and divine right. Louis XIV's passion for diamonds, and the discovery of the Golconda diamond mines in India, only amplified the extravagance at Versailles. The aristocracy needed little encouragement to engage in such display: diamonds adorned everything from buttons and fans to sword hilts and hair ornaments. Men wore almost as many jewels as women, from powdered wigs scattered with gemstones to waistcoats trimmed with gold and rubies. Women's pieces were often large and formal: tiered necklaces, stomacher brooches, and girdles of diamonds worn over silk gowns. Under Louis XV, a lighter, more decorative style emerged, featuring floral motifs, asymmetry, and enamel miniatures. Stone-cutting techniques also improved, introducing the brilliant cut, allowing for more sparkle in finer settings. Few courtly jewels survive intact today. Many were broken up or refashioned after the Revolution, but examples can still be found in museum collections and occasionally at higher-end auctions.

A French drapery-style necklace in yellow gold, adorned with floral motifs and set with sapphire cabochons, accompanied by a sapphire and diamond ring and painted cameo brooch.

L O
Relative à la vérification des compt
trésor publi
Donné à Paris, le
LOUIS, par la grâce
lle de l'État, Roi des
L'Assemblée
ordonnons ce qui
a décré
du 3 Juillet
l'an quatrièm
après
rdinaire des fina
que l'établis
ur objet la vérif
nent du b
ens du trésor
on des comptes
ar la promp
ic, il ne peut être en pleine acti-
ces justificat
ise de leurs comptes respectifs,
dernier au 1.er
fixé par la loi
soumissions de
res et conditions
u que cin-
de leurs apureme
mptes, et
également que
lus grand
ont offert la reddi
des pays
ite depuis leur prése
ptes, sont
il est instar
Jouannin
BAYONNE

Restoration and Louis Philippe (1815–1848)

Following the fall of the First Empire (1804–1815), a new wave of Romanticism shaped French jewelry. Designs became lighter and more refined, placing greater importance—and value—on the jeweler's skill. Pearls were in vogue and cameos in high demand. Women layered bracelets, wore ornate belt buckles, and favored intricate earrings.

Second Empire and industrialization (1840–1880)

Second Empire (1852–1870) jewelry was characterized by a revival of grandeur and opulence under Napoleon III and Empress Eugénie. Their taste for lavish display set the tone for Parisian society, where galas and receptions demanded ever more spectacular parures. Diamonds and richly colored gems were mounted in profusion onto tiaras, necklaces, brooches, and earrings, and enriched with enamel for an ostentatious effect.

From the mid-nineteenth century, technical advances led to the gradual reshaping of the French jewelry landscape. Improved stamping and casting techniques made it possible to produce fine-looking pieces more affordably. Paris and Lyon became major centers for this new wave of production, offering beautifully made adaptations of older designs. Popular motifs like garlands, anchors, and sacred hearts were no longer limited to custom commissions and the elite, and could now circulate widely. Designs responded in kind, becoming lighter, more geometric, and easier to wear.

The formalization of schooling in jewelry making in the 1860s marked another turning point. The Chambre Syndicale de la Bijouterie-Joaillerie insisted that students needed not only technical apprenticeships but also artistic

ABOVE, LEFT
A French nineteenth-century gold brooch set with an agate cameo; a horn hair ornament topped with a star set with rhinestones; and a nineteenth-century pendant necklace featuring a rose and silver gold arrow.

ABOVE, RIGHT
A Napoleon III-style yellow gold and silver Milanese mesh cuff bracelet set with a citrine and diamonds, produced in France.

ABOVE, LEFT
A rose gold and silver crescent moon brooch from the Napoleon III period, with a full pavé setting of old-cut and rose-cut diamonds.

ABOVE, RIGHT
An art deco ladies watch, with a nineteenth-century cameo brooch.

training to work as jewelers. The Conservatoire des Arts et Métiers in Paris introduced sketching and modeling classes, which would become the foundation for generations of artisans, ensuring that creativity remained at the heart of French jewelry design, even as production scaled up.

Belle époque (1890–1914)

Considered the golden age of French jewelry, this era of peace in Europe gave rise to new creativity and a desire for beauty. Belle époque designs were feminine and lightweight, often featuring floral and ribbon motifs fashioned from gold and platinum. Precious stones and pearls were used in abundance, arranged in delicate settings, set into ornate tiaras, or gathered in long necklaces that caught the light. The greatest French jewelers took up residence on Place Vendôme in Paris, and their ambitions were tangible. While pieces from this period are often described as romantic and refined, they were also highly technical. Many were transformable, with hidden clasps and detachable elements that allowed a brooch to become a pendant or a necklace to be worn in several different ways.

Art nouveau (1895–1910)

Running parallel to the belle époque, the art nouveau movement offered a more sensual alternative to the classical vocabulary of garlands and bows. Designers turned away from symmetry, and instead drew inspiration from the natural world, replicating peacock feathers, orchids, or dragonflies. Influenced by the popular Arts & Crafts movement that swept through Europe, French art nouveau jewelry developed a distinctive softness and fluidity. It favored organic materials like horn, enamel, and opals, chosen for their sheen and translucence as much as for their color. Produced in small quantities and often signed, these

pieces, unfortunately, were not built to last, so well-preserved examples are rare. When found intact—typically in Parisian collections—they remain some of the most poetic and sought-after jewels on the market.

Art deco (1920–1935)

After World War I, France, like the United States, entered a period of prosperity—and with it came a renewed appetite for glamour. Lavish parties, modern silhouettes, and a fascination with speed defined the era. Glass and paste jewelry—known today as cocktail or costume jewelry—became popular as a stylish, affordable way to dress up. Among the wealthy, however, diamonds never went out of fashion. Platinum mounts held emeralds, sapphires, and diamonds in crisp, geometric compositions. Rings featured elongated baguette or navette cuts; brooches and tiaras echoed the symmetry of modern architecture. Pearls remained a staple, while onyx, jade, and coral added bold color contrasts.

Mid-century (1940–1960)

During the Occupation, materials were scarce and styles became conservative. However, by the 1950s a new wave of glamour had emerged. Designers embraced bold silhouettes, such as voluminous brooches, oversized cocktail rings, and articulated bracelets. Gold returned with a vengeance, often sculpted into heavy woven textures or set with semiprecious stones. French costume jewelry also gained momentum, championed by designers such as Dior and Chanel, who understood that elegance need not be dictated by material alone, but depended just as much on line, balance, and intention. Many mid-century pieces—both fine and costume—remain highly collectible for their exuberance and wearability.

ABOVE, LEFT
An art deco ring from the 1930s in white gold and platinum, set at the center with an old-cut diamond.

ABOVE, RIGHT
A coral necklace and hair comb from the nineteenth century.

FACING PAGE
A selection of nineteenth-century *poissarde* and *dormeuse* earrings in their original boxes.

PALAIS-ROYAL
35 R.
LANGRES

OR 750/1000
4G.B.
850€
380€
600€

Regional Specialties

After the Revolution, gold jewelry was no longer the preserve of aristocrats. In regions like Normandy, Alsace, Provence, and parts of Brittany, rising rural wealth meant landowners and merchants could commission jewelry for their wives and daughters. These regional pieces often evolved from simple forms—crosses and lockets, which were gradually adapted into shapes specific to a town, valley, or coastline. These were not items made to follow trends—they were family heirlooms, showcasing local craftsmanship and materials. Their survival often depended on the following generation, and on whether a daughter liked a piece enough to wear it, cherished it enough to keep it, or found herself in need and forced to sell it. Thanks to their emotional value—far greater than their weight in gold—many pieces have survived intact today.

Of particular note are the many designs of religious crosses—one of the most popular items of French regional jewelry—which varied from one area to another. A cross from the Manche département in Normandy, for instance, might appear heavy and stylized, but more delicate and elongated further south. In French Catalonia, garnets became emblematic, and the city of Perpignan was celebrated for its particular cut of the stone. In Dieppe, ivory carving flourished, and the nineteenth century saw the spread of fashionable hatpins, embellished with semi-precious stones. In the north, the prosperity of the fishing trade also left its mark. Fishermen's wives, eager to display their financial success, wore gold earrings called *milanos*, featuring an interlinked design that is reminiscent of the structure of fishing nets.

Today, there are few places where traditional jewelry is as visible as in the city of Arles, in Provence. Here, the traditional costume is still honored and is always accompanied by jewelry with deep historical roots. Its signature piece is the *croix Jeannette*, thought by some to date back to Queen Jeanne in the fourteenth century. Its symbolism is precise: the gold base represents the sun (man), the silver settings the moon (woman), and the diamonds bind the two for eternity. Other adornments include *poissardes* earrings, inspired by Marseille fishmongers, and *dormeuses*, named for their elongated clasps. The *coulas*—a three-ring bracelet worn high on the arm—recalls Gallo-Roman origins. Later, the *cicada* brooch—immortalized by poet Frédéric Mistral—emerged as a badge of Provençal identity. For centuries, Arlésiennes have supported local goldsmiths, ensuring that these symbolic jewels continue to shine as a vital part of Provence's cultural heritage.

FACING PAGE
A display of brooches and traditional regional crosses from the eighteenth and nineteenth centuries.

PAGE 140
A gold serpent necklace with turquoise enamel and fine pearls, dating from c. 1860, paired with a vintage scarab ring featuring engraved enameled steatite.

PAGE 141
A nineteenth-century articulated bracelet from Sicily, in yellow and rose gold with amber cabochons, alongside earrings with a cannetille setting.

MEET THE EXPERT

Camille Cuvelier

Galerie Pénélope, Paris
galeriepenelope.com
@galeriepenelope

A rare gem among dealers, Camille Cuvelier is a specialist in antique jewelry. She founded Galerie Pénélope in 2019 and has been captivating buyers and collectors with her exceptional selection and curation of restored heirlooms ever since.

The boutique operates primarily online, allowing Camille to connect with clients around the world, who can browse her glittering portfolio from the comfort of their home, while benefiting from her expert advice. For those seeking a more tactile experience, Camille welcomes visits by appointment at her Paris showroom, located in the heart of Montmartre. Her stand can also be found at in-person events, including the Chatou antique fair. Whether in person or remotely, she always takes great care to offer individual guidance to each of her patrons.

After refining her expertise in a Parisian antique jewelry shop, and later at the prestigious French jeweler Chaumet, she set out on her own, first gaining traction on Etsy before launching her brand. Her dedication has earned her recognition, with her pieces featured in fashion editorials for *Vogue* and *Vanity Fair*, and in popular television series like *Bridgerton*.

Seeking out pieces with symbolic meaning is her favorite part of the job, and she travels the length of Europe visiting antique dealers, jewelers, auction houses, and other suppliers in her network to find the most unique jewels, trace provenance, identify mysterious stones, and uncover hidden signatures.

CAMILLE'S TIPS

It is of utmost importance to work with a dealer you trust. Antique jewelry is an emotional investment, and having someone who understands your taste, budget, and questions makes all the difference when it comes to balancing aesthetic desires and practical needs. Invest in a small loupe or magnifying glass to check a piece's hallmark and verify its authenticity. Finally, wear your pieces. Well-made jewelry is meant to be enjoyed; with proper care, it can last for generations, and even damaged items can often be beautifully restored.

AMIENS

The Collector's Eye

If you're considering buying antique jewelry, the first step is to seek out a professional and trustworthy dealer. Ideally, they should be a certified gemologist or, at the very least, highly knowledgeable about the pieces they sell. A reputable dealer should be able to speak confidently about the piece's materials, period, and construction—so don't be shy about requesting details.

In France, if an antique dealer sells a piece made of precious metal—gold, silver, or platinum—it has to be hallmarked. If the item is not already marked, it must be tested and stamped by the Bureau des Douanes (French customs authorities) before sale. French hallmarks are relatively easy to learn. French gold is typically marked with an eagle's head (for 18k), scallop shell (for 14k), or clover (for 9k), silver with a Minerva head, and platinum with a dog's head. Pieces with lower percentages might bear the stamp "ET," and gold and silver of foreign or uncertain origin are stamped with an owl or swan respectively. Since jewelry dealers, both at fairs and in stores, are regularly inspected in France, you can feel reasonably assured of your purchase. That said, there is a gray area for items under 3 grams in weight, which, by law, are not required to be hallmarked. For more valuable purchases, always ask for a certificate of authenticity or a written guarantee from the dealer, and avoid buying unmarked items.

Antique pieces from the great French jewelry houses are few and far between on the market, but these *maisons* do, on occasion, release vintage or historic designs for sale. Many auction houses also specialize in antique jewels, but it is always worthwhile approaching a house directly first. The most reputable names include Chaumet, Boucheron, Cartier, Van Cleef & Arpels, Mauboussin, and Hermès.

If you plan to invest in antique jewelry more extensively, consider expanding your knowledge. L'École des Arts Joailliers, Van Cleef & Arpels's school of jewelry arts in Paris, offers excellent courses, including one-day workshops focused on gem setting, stone identification, and historical techniques. A little technical knowledge goes a long way and can help you spot not only quality, but rarity and craftsmanship. You may also like to purchase a small jeweler's loupe or lens, so you can take a closer look at stones and hallmarks.

The trick to antique jewelry is learning how to style together pieces from different eras.

Caring for Antique Jewelry

As far as antique jewelry is concerned, the key to longevity lies in its care. These pieces, with their exquisite craftsmanship and long history, demand more attention than their modern counterparts, even if they have been restored.

Common sense also dictates when it is best to take off rings, bracelets, and necklaces. Chemicals can damage both metals and stones, and it's important to remove jewelry during any manual or sporting activity, or when showering or swimming.

Stones—especially those set in delicate claws—can shift or become loose over time. A useful tip: shake your jewelry near your ear. If you hear a small noise, it may mean the stone is loose and it is time to stop wearing the piece and visit a jeweler—the sooner, the better. A jeweler can also resize rings, but keep in mind that fingers change size over time and with the seasons. A ring that fits perfectly in winter may feel tight in summer, and that's completely normal.

While gold and diamonds are generally durable, they still need attention. Diamonds don't scratch easily, but they can break if struck against something hard, like a tile or sink, so take care to remove your jewelry before performing any heavy tasks. To clean gold and diamond jewelry, it is recommended that you gently soak your pieces in hot (not boiling) water with a little dish soap overnight, which can help restore shine. Do not use a toothbrush while cleaning, as this can dislodge stones by disturbing the claws. Depending on the piece, a jeweler can also clean it using an ultrasound bath.

Enamel, emeralds, opals, and other colored stones need extra care. Enamel is especially fragile, and colored stones are prone to heat damage, so avoid hot water, direct sunlight, or exposing them to extreme conditions. If they could do with cleaning, it's best to consult a professional to ensure they are handled properly.

Pearls also benefit from regular care. To preserve their luster, avoid exposure to heat, water, and especially perfumes or skincare products containing alcohol, which can erode their surface. A gentle rub with a soft cloth and a drop of a natural body oil (such as argon oil) will keep them shining wonderfully. Loose pearl necklaces and bracelets can also be rethreaded—new knots create a slightly stiffer setting that helps to prevent rubbing and chipping.

Some jewelry is especially susceptible to friction and shocks. Bracelets can easily become scratched or dented if you're not careful, and chains can weaken if overloaded with heavy pendants. If a chain link breaks, it can be repaired, but it is unlikely to be as strong as it once was. To prevent the weakening of links, avoid direct contact with perfume, especially on silver chains, which can also be tarnished by the alcohol.

Finally, some fashion accessories, such as scarves, can be the undoing of jeweled necklaces and earrings, as they can easily catch on prongs and damage delicate settings. Claw settings will naturally catch on fine fabrics from time to time, but if it starts happening more frequently, it is worth having a jeweler check for raised edges or worn claws that could be smoothed down.

FACING PAGE
Nineteenth-century earrings, necklace, and ring in garnet, typical of the region around Arles.

PAGES 146–147
A selection of vintage jewelry dating from the 1920s to the 1980s.

PAGES 148–149
A wide selection of vintage and costume jewelry at the Sunday fair in Carpentras, in the south of France.

MEET THE EXPERT

Julie Mialet

Pierres de Julie, Paris
lespierresdejulie.com
@pierresdejulie

Raised in a family that cherished history and beauty, Julie Mialet grew up in Paris, surrounded by art, antiques, and culture. She fostered a lasting appreciation for craftsmanship from an early age. After studying luxury gastronomy and embarking on a career in hospitality in London, Julie unexpectedly found her true calling—fine jewelry—during a visit to Idar-Oberstein, Germany's historic gemstone-cutting capital. She returned to Paris to pursue formal training, obtaining her diploma from the Institut National de Gemmologie in 2004. Shortly thereafter, she opened her boutique-gallery, dedicated to antique and vintage jewelry, as well as bespoke creations, in Paris's 15th arrondissement.

Specializing in rare gemstones and vintage pieces, Julie offers a highly personalized service that includes expert appraisals, transformations (new pieces created from antique components), and custom designs. Her respect for the story behind each stone or piece ensures that every creation is both meaningful and honed to perfection. Clients also benefit from her ability to certify stones through renowned laboratories, such as Laboratoire Français Gemmologie (LFG).

With a well-established international network and a distinctly French savoir faire, Les Pierres de Julie brings new life to antique treasures, while imagining contemporary pieces that always feel considered, individual, and enduring.

JULIE'S TIPS

Vintage jewelry has great character. Be bold in the pieces you wear, and don't be afraid to mix colors. If you are fortunate enough to inherit a piece but it doesn't fit your style, then look at options for reworking the stones to create a bespoke piece—you'll be amazed by the results.

OUVRANT PL OR 70€
OUVRANT PL OR 135€
ARG. AGATHE 45€
OUVRANT PL ANCIEN 25€
OUVRANT PL OR 50€
BROCHE NACRE 20€
OUVRANT PL OR 45€
MET ART 25€
ARG
PENDENTIF vermeil AR/OR. 30€ 1024 HUGO
BROCHE ARG 35

ARG 35€
ARG Hematites 25€
PLOR Email 20€
Pendentif PLOR 20€
25€
ARG Art Nouveau 35€
ARG
Nous Revenons

CHAPTER 8

Chandeliers and Mirrors

While we all understand the importance of lighting in interior design, its application can make or break a room, as anyone who has seen the sparkling effect of a crystal chandelier will tell you. Crystal pendants on vast chandeliers are an effective and beautiful way to diffuse gentle light. Whether designed for tapered candles or adapted for electric bulbs, their faceted droplets scatter and magnify illumination, while strategically placed mirrors further expand and diffuse the light throughout a space.

A striking demonstration of this can be found at the Château de Versailles, where, under Louis XIV, candles were the sole source of light—luxurious beeswax was reserved for the royal apartments, while smoky tallow lit the common spaces. With each candle burning for only a few hours, an army of attendants was required to keep the château aglow. Since candlelight provides only limited brightness, even en masse, eighteenth-century designers began incorporating glass and crystal pendants into chandeliers. Acting as prisms, they caught and multiplied each flame, creating a brighter effect.

Today, we no longer exclusively rely on candles, but the play of light on glass is still captivating. A well-placed mirror or chandelier can transform a room, enhancing its atmosphere and creating a sense of volume. Consider, too, fixtures other than overhead chandeliers: an antique crystal sconce or decorated candelabra can create an equally dramatic effect.

A late eighteenth-century Italian lantern and a nineteenth-century Italian chandelier originally from a church.

Chandelier Styles

Antique chandeliers are typically ornate and decorated, made from materials such as brass, copper, or bronze. Older examples may have glass shades surrounding each candlestick, to protect the flame from drafts.

Lustre corbeille

This design is basket-shaped, with strands of glass or crystal draped upwards from a central ring, forming an airy, open weave.

Lustre montgolfière

Shaped like a hot-air balloon, this style features a rounded body tapering at top and bottom, densely strung with crystals.

Appliques

These are wall-mounted sconces, often sporting trailing crystals and intricate, nature-inspired metalwork.

Lustre cage

Built around a visible metal, cage-like framework, this design allows for a more sculptural display of candle arms and crystal drops.

Lustre à 5, 6, 7, 8 bras

The name for the classic multi-arm chandelier, typically with five or more curved branches radiating from a central stem, each holding a candle or bulb.

Lustre à lacet

This is characterized by delicate wirework or ribbon-like metal details entwined with crystal, creating a lighter, more decorative silhouette.

ABOVE, LEFT
A magnificent eight-branch chandelier.

ABOVE, RIGHT
A nineteenth-century bronze and crystal chandelier—a special commission by Baccarat.

FACING PAGE
Above the table hangs a pair of metal and porcelain chandeliers dating from the early 1900s.

Mirror Styles

Trumeau

Tall and often rectangular, this design typically features a painted or carved panel above the glass, and was originally integrated into the architecture of a wall.

Miroir à parcloses, or marginal mirror

Typically dating from the seventeenth to eighteenth centuries, this is defined by a central mirror and a mirrored border, divided by gilded or painted wooden moldings.

Louis XIV (1660–1715)

Monumental, symmetrical, and bold, this style usually features a heavy frame, with thick gilding, strong vertical lines, and classical ornamentation.

Louis XV / rococo (1730–1760s)

Highly romantic in style, this type of mirror is arched and features asymmetrical curves, delicate floral carvings, and shell or scroll motifs. The gilded frames are ornate yet airy, with a sense of movement and fluidity.

Louis XVI (1760–1790s)

This era saw a return to symmetry and neoclassical restraint, with rectangular or oval shapes, finely gilded frames, architectural lines, and occasional rosettes or inset mirror panels.

Empire (1804–1830)

While rectangular and oval mirrors remain the dominant shape, their decorative elements are bolder. Corner medallions, carved eagles, and structural details like columns or double frames are common, along with black paintwork and silver or gold gilding.

Louis Philippe (1830–1848)

Quietly refined and very versatile, Louis Philippe mirrors are distinguished by their soft, rounded corners and absence of overt decoration. Frames are typically gilded or silvered, often finished with a slim beaded inner trim.

Soleil, or sunburst (mid-twentieth century)

A twentieth-century revival of the Sun King's motif, these circular mirrors radiate gold or bronze rays and are usually relatively small in scale. Some examples may technically be vintage rather than antique, but they are just as popular.

Carved wooden frames on nineteenth-century French mirrors.

The Collector's Eye

Chandeliers

If you're trying to estimate the age of a chandelier, one basic detail can help: a solid central stem typically indicates that the chandelier was made before the advent of electricity. If the central tube is hollow, this suggests a later piece, designed to conceal wiring for electric bulbs; however, older chandeliers have sometimes been adapted for this purpose.

When selecting a chandelier for your home, it is essential to consider its weight. Even simple designs can be surprisingly heavy. This is important when deciding where to hang it—you need to make sure you can do so safely—but also when arranging transport, as shipping costs are based on both volume and weight.

While learning how to define age and style will help refine your taste, it unfortunately doesn't dictate a chandelier's price. Worth is typically based on the reputation of the maker, with names like Saint-Louis and Baccarat being the most renowned. Size, materials, and craftsmanship also affect the final cost. The number of facets on a crystal or glass drop, for instance, directly affects how much light it reflects, making a piece more or less desirable. Monograms add another layer of interest. Antique Baccarat chandeliers often feature a red octagonal hallmark, while ecclesiastical pieces may bear initials such as *M* for Marie, *IHS* (Iesus Hominum Salvator), or even small crosses etched into the prisms.

Cut or blown crystal is also more expensive than mass-produced pieces, but distinguishing crystal from glass can be tricky. A few clues will help reveal the material's authenticity. Real crystal has a faint gray tint due to its lead content, and blue reflections when held up to the light. It also tends to be more brilliant and transparent than glass. If you clink two prisms together, genuine crystal emits a clear, high-pitched ring. A final clue is the weight—crystal is heavier than glass.

To verify the type of metal used, there are a few simple tests that can help. Antique bronze chandeliers are typically more valuable than their imitations, and scratching a discreet spot with something sharp can reveal the underlying metal. A yellowish hue indicates bronze, while a silvery one suggests a less valuable alloy. If scratching isn't possible, look for existing wear along the edges, which often exposes the true metal beneath. Tapping the body can also be telling: bronze emits a clear, high-pitched tone, while babbitt—a popular alloy—sounds dull when struck. Lastly, since bronze oxidizes over time, it develops a distinctive, rich patina, which not only adds depth and interest to a piece, but is also a great signifier of age and authenticity.

A splendid nineteenth-century chandelier comprising hexagonal prisms and multi-faceted ball-shaped crystal tears.

Mirrors

Antique mirrors, typically made before the early twentieth century, offer more than just reflection. They carry the marks of their time, both in craftsmanship and condition. Mirrors dating to the eighteenth century are rare, since many were destroyed during the French Revolution; nineteenth-century examples are more common.

The Industrial Revolution made it easier to replicate artisanal designs, so careful inspection is key to assessing an antique mirror's authenticity. Many on the market today are made to look antique or combine genuine vintage frames with replacement glass. This might be due to damage to the original mirror plate or a desire for a clearer reflection. However, for a mirror to be considered truly antique, it should be at least one hundred years old and produced before mass manufacturing became the norm.

The glass itself is revealing. Antique mirrors typically show their age through slight imperfections on the glass plate, like creases, waviness, air bubbles, or small spots. All of these irregularities are the result of older production methods, and are not considered flaws. In fact, they are often sought after as desirable features and key indicators of authenticity.

Another detail to check is the presence of a maker's mark. This may be stamped or labeled on the back of the frame, or placed discreetly elsewhere if the mirror is part of a dressing table or larger piece of furniture. These marks help identify the maker and the approximate date of production.

ABOVE, LEFT
Bamboo-framed mirrors in different shapes and sizes create an effective display when hung together.

ABOVE, RIGHT
Mirror specialists generally have a wide selection on offer.

FACING PAGE
At the Foire de Chatou, there are always plenty of large wall and trumeau mirrors to be found.

Caring for Chandeliers and Mirrors

Chandeliers

The biggest concern with chandeliers is their fragility. Glass and crystal can easily shatter if not protected properly for transport. If you're buying from a serious antique dealer who offers to prepare the chandelier for shipping, ask if all the crystals are going to be removed and wrapped separately, and if so, to provide instructions for reassembly.

For the best protection during shipping, a chandelier should travel in a purpose-built wooden crate, and hang from the inner ceiling of the crate. Regardless of whether the crystal pendants are removed, there should be adequate padding around the chandelier to protect the structure.

Cleaning a crystal chandelier takes a few simple steps. First, remove any accumulated dust using a microfiber cloth or feather duster. Next, detach the crystals from the chandelier, to allow for better cleaning, taking photos beforehand to help with reassembly. Then, wash each crystal drop in lukewarm water with some liquid dish soap. You can also add a little white vinegar to this solution for a stronger clean. Rinse in clear water and dry carefully with a soft cloth while wearing gloves to avoid leaving fingerprints.

If the chandelier frame is bronze, it will naturally gather patina with age. To restore its original shine, you can gently polish it with a soft cloth and a small amount of metal polish designed for bronze, but avoid harsh abrasives to preserve the integrity of the material.

ABOVE, LEFT AND RIGHT
Details of crystals on antique chandeliers.

FACING PAGE
In addition to the size and shape of the crystals, the color and design of the frame also contribute to creating a beautiful chandelier.

FACING PAGE
A carved crown of leaves with a bow tops a beaded mirror frame.

ABOVE, LEFT
An eighteenth-century mirror in a style known as Beaucaire.

ABOVE, RIGHT
Late eighteenth-century mirrors.

PAGE 164
Philippe Provot offers an eclectic mix of eighteenth-century antiques.

PAGE 165
This spectacular chandelier stands nearly six and a half feet (two meters) tall and requires meticulous care and patience when handling and hanging.

PAGES 166–167
Antique dealers display chandeliers in groups, with or without light bulbs.

Mirrors

If you find a mirror in poor condition, be wary of attempting restoration work yourself, as this can devalue or further damage the mirror. In some cases, the mirror may be worth more in its current state, so it is always advisable to consult an expert. Defective glass may not need to be fully replaced.

Spots or misty patches caused by de-silvering (when the silver backing wears away, often due to moisture) can be improved by having the backing re-silvered by a professional. Be mindful, though, that this could accentuate any flaws or scratches on the glass. Older mirrors may still have their original mercury backing, which can deteriorate and pose a health risk if disturbed or broken. However, as long as the mirror is intact, the risk is minimal. When buying an antique mirror, check the backing's condition and ask the seller about the materials used. If uncertain, consult a specialist to test for mercury.

For best upkeep, position framed mirrors away from direct sunlight and heat sources like radiators, to prevent the wood from drying, splitting, or fading. Avoid harsh or abrasive cleaning products, as these can damage both the frame and the glass. Simple methods work best to remove dust and dirt. Start by dusting the frame with a clean microfiber cloth and a soft brush to reach intricate areas. Next, clean the glass with a solution of one part white vinegar and two parts water, working it over the glass in circular motions. Buff dry using a clean cloth. The frame can be wiped with a damp cloth, then carefully patted dry. For wooden frames, you may want to use a wax or cream polish to finish.

MEET THE EXPERT

Philippe Provot

Brocante de Balines
Verneuil-sur-Avre, Normandy
@brocantedebalines

Raised in a historic manor house in Normandy, Philippe developed an eye for architectural detail early on. He began as a young craftsman restoring his parents' home, gaining firsthand experience in traditional building techniques. His practical knowledge quickly expanded and he soon found himself called upon to repair and renovate other family residences in the region.

When Philippe met Annette, an established antique dealer in Normandy, their shared passion for heritage and design sparked both a romance and a working partnership. Annette introduced him to the rich and varied world of French antiques and *brocantes*, and together they built a reputation as knowledgeable and trustworthy dealers, honing their expertise the old-fashioned way: scouring estate clearances, researching obscure pieces in dusty volumes, and traveling across regions to consult specialists long before online marketplaces or forums existed.

In 1997, Philippe cofounded the antique collective known as Balines, named for the nearby village. Housed in a large former warehouse that he and a partner initially rented, then purchased, Balines has since grown into a respected hub of a dozen dealers, each with a distinctive specialty. Philippe's own aesthetic leans naturally toward the elegance of the eighteenth century. He is drawn to rococo design and is known for his ever-changing collection of chandeliers, gilded mirrors, paintings, and period furniture. Clients value not only his eye but his integrity; many return regularly and often commission him to source specific pieces.

Beyond his role as a dealer, Philippe remains deeply connected to architectural restoration. His own home has been lovingly extended in genuine eighteenth-century style—a testament to his belief in authenticity.

PHILIPPE'S TIPS

Every piece that passes through Philippe's hands is treated with the same philosophy: retain what's original, repair what's essential, and let the age show where it can speak for itself.

12
Rexall
The Best Known
Name in Drugs
6

CHAPTER 9

Furniture

The distinctive French country style can only be achieved through a skillful mix of old and new. True French country homes are never furnished entirely in the latest trend. Instead, they come together over the years, composed of a combination of family hand-me-downs, purchases from favorite stores, and a generous dose of time-honored furniture and accessories. Today, these older elements are often vintage rather than antique—mixing mid-century furniture with contemporary décor has become extremely popular in recent years—and the effect is both highly personal and incredibly pleasing.

So, what continues to draw us to antique furniture? Patina is the first word that comes to mind. A richly polished wood finish or a beautifully faded painted piece brings much more character to a room than any new item could ever hope to convey. Quality and resistance are additional winning factors. A table or bedhead crafted more than a hundred years ago has already proven it can stand the test of time. There is so much pleasure in giving it a new home and allowing it to set the tone in a different setting.

Furniture passed down from generation to generation can provide special enjoyment, since it is imbued with family history, but pieces from an antique or *brocante* dealer often come with their own story, too. Buying your own pieces also allows you to explore the vast range of antique furniture on offer—what delights one person may leave another cold. In any case, it is always a good idea to brush up on some defining features before hitting the market.

Moreover, despite growing efforts to protect architectural heritage, there are still moments when a property is refurbished with little regard for its original features, and the existing parquet floors, paving stones, and even wooden paneling for entire rooms can end up on the antique market.

Yet not all salvage is born of neglect. In many ways, it is a poetic form of preservation. While some old homes are dismantled, others are simply beyond repair, but their parts can be rescued, reused by respectful renovators, or reimagined in new settings. A former pair of window shutters might be used indoors as closet doors in a guest room. Old tiles can be reinstalled in small spaces like powder rooms or entryways, making a strong design statement.

An eighteenth-century French oak dresser with a metal mesh finish on the doors.

Furniture Design Periods

Baroque (1600–1750)

Dramatic and high contrast, baroque furniture is characterized by heavy carvings and opulent gilding. Twisted columns, exaggerated details, and sculptural forms create a sense of harmony and movement in these pieces, while exotic woods and metalwork add an air of grandeur.

Louis XIII (1610–1643)

Furniture from this period is heavy, with a slightly architectural feel. Dark woods like oak and walnut dominate, and designs feature geometric carvings and straight, turned legs. Upholstered pieces typically come in rich fabrics like velvet and tapestry, often studded with nailhead trim.

Louis XIV (1643–1710)

Defined by grandeur and symmetry, Louis XIV furniture reflects the opulence of Versailles and the era's growing interest in interior design. Think gilded wood, intricate marquetry, and bronze mounts. Decorative features—sun motifs and acanthus leaves—and rich materials like ebony and tortoiseshell are de rigueur.

Régence (1715–1723)

Albeit short, this period marked an important transition from the rigidity of Louis XIV style to the fluidity of Louis XV. French regency furniture introduced softer lines and more comfort. The style features cabriole legs, chinoiserie, and wood veneers, while ornamentation tends toward the delicate and asymmetrical.

ABOVE, LEFT
The early nineteenth-century gold framed paintings on the wall form an attractive contrast with the twentieth-century sofa and armchair below.

ABOVE, RIGHT
A nineteenth-century painted screen stands behind a Napoleon III sofa reupholstered in blush silk.

FACING PAGE
A pair of early nineteenth-century chairs showing signs of wear still maintain their beauty.

Louis XV (1725–1760)

Also known as *rocaille*, rococo, or Pompadour style, Louis XV furniture is curvaceous, asymmetrical, and highly decorative. Look for extravagant details like floral marquetry and soft pastel upholstery—a nod to the era's whimsical taste.

Louis XVI (1750–1790)

This style displays a return to neoclassicism, bringing straight lines, symmetry, and fluted legs. Furniture is refined and elegant, with carved garlands, medallions, and ribbons. Mahogany, lighter woods, and painted finishes dominate.

Directoire (1792–1804)

Marked by Revolutionary sobriety, Directoire furniture remains neoclassical in style, but strips away excess, favoring clean lines and classical forms. Mahogany and painted wood are common, accented by elegant brass details.

Empire (1804–1815)

Napoleon's reign brought a new level of theatricality to interiors. Empire furniture is imposing, symmetrical, and heavily adorned with imperial symbols: laurel wreaths, eagles, sphinxes, and dramatic architectural elements inspired by Ancient Rome and Egypt. Mahogany and gilt accents enhance the stately aura of these pieces.

Restoration (1814–1839)

With the return of the monarchy, furniture designs softened, moving away from the rigidity of the Empire epoch. Curved forms, plush seating, and rich veneers in rosewood and mahogany define the style, and pieces are often accented with inlaid mother-of-pearl or brass for a more intimate, inviting feel.

Louis Philippe (1830–1848)

Louis Philippe furniture is practical, comfortable, and unpretentious. While less decorative, it remains elegant thanks to its polished restraint; veneered woods, rounded corners, and simple scroll feet replace earlier ornamental features.

An antique Swedish chest of drawers, painted in a distinctive gray-blue, stands behind an early nineteenth-century daybed reupholstered in blue linen.

Napoleon III (1852–1870)

Napoleon III style borrows freely from past eras—Gothic, Renaissance, rococo, and Empire all reappear in new forms. Pieces true to this style feature black lacquered pear wood, mother-of-pearl inlays, and upholstered seats, creating a theatrical aesthetic. This period also saw the rise of rattan furniture, used to furnish the newly popular winter salons. Imported from Asia, this material immediately seduced the European and American public, and rattan was used for seating, tables, and a myriad of smaller decorative items.

Art nouveau (1895–1910)

Inspired by nature, art nouveau furniture features flowing lines, leafy motifs, and asymmetry. Exotic woods, stained glass, and wrought-iron details seamlessly intertwine. The result is a flowing, decorative style that moves away from classical rigidity.

Art deco (1925–1940)

Emerging from the 1925 International Exhibition of Decorative Arts, art deco style embodies sleek luxury. Craftsmanship and machine-age aesthetics combine, resulting in furniture that features bold geometry, streamlined forms, and rich materials, from lacquer and chrome to ivory and glass.

Mid-century (1950–1960)

With warm wood tones, sleek lines, and minimal ornamentation, mid-century design displays the influence of Scandinavian and American innovations. Blending new materials like plywood, fiberglass, and aluminum with softer, organic structures, these pieces bring modernism into daily life.

ABOVE, LEFT
A Louis XIV chest of drawers makes a perfect setting for small collections of china or paintings.

ABOVE, RIGHT
Directoire-style sofas are perfectly proportioned for today's hallways.

FACING PAGE
A complete set of 1940s wicker chairs with upholstered seats and backrests on display at Lila K at the Marché Paul Bert in Saint-Ouen.

PAGE 176
A Perret & Vibert cane sofa with turquoise details from the 1860s is paired with a striking circular rattan mirror by Artémon Création, Galerie Vauclair's own design line.

PAGE 177
A nineteenth-century cane and rattan winter garden chair by Perret & Vibert and a set of majolica plates create a charming vignette.

MEET THE EXPERT

Laurence Vauclair

Galerie Vauclair
Paris and Marché Paul Bert,
Puces de Saint-Ouen
galerie-vauclair.fr
@galerievauclair

Laurence Vauclair has spent decades buying and selling antiques. Her parents' love for antiques and museums instilled in her an early appreciation for old world charm, which her family nurtured with long slow summers spent in the picturesque countryside of Touraine, surrounded by forests and natural beauty. Rather than pursue traditional studies, she and her first partner traveled across France, scouting for exceptional pieces that would soon grace her gallery. Laurence credits her success to these trips, during which she was able to collect antiques while also gaining an intimate knowledge of the various regions of France and the tastes of its local people.

Since founding Galerie Vauclair in 1993, she has built a reputation for timeless interior design pieces. She has represented France at antique fairs worldwide and now runs two elegant boutiques: one at the Marché Paul Bert at the Puces de Saint-Ouen—the flea market just outside Paris—and another in the capital's prestigious Saint-Germain-des-Prés neighborhood.

Laurence and her husband, Denis, are known for their mesmerizing displays, styled to resemble French salons, which captivate audiences worldwide with their distinctive use of Napoleonic art and wicker furniture. The latter is a particular favorite of Laurence, whose work often harmonizes interior design and nature, evoking her true refuge: the countryside. Laurence specializes in ceramics, including sought-after Palissy and majolica ware, and has collaborated with esteemed brands such as Hermès, Cartier, Pierre Frey, and more, bearing testimony to her influence in the field.

LAURENCE'S TIPS

Diving into the world of antique acquisitions—whether it be for business or pleasure—needn't require a lavish budget. The important thing is to embrace your distinctive style and stay true to it.

The Collector's Eye

Good quality antique furniture should last a lifetime—and beyond—so it's important to consider your purchases carefully, only buying pieces that really speak to you. Try to imagine where they will feel at home in your space, what function they will serve, and whether they meet your current needs. When shopping at a dealer's store, bring photos and measurements of your space—dealers can often offer helpful, unexpected insights.

Although surfaces can be reupholstered and cushions can be refilled, always take the time to test joints, by gently rocking them to see if they move. Repairing a joint can sometimes prove to be a larger and more costly challenge than anticipated.

Pay special attention to the condition of wicker seating or rattan-backed chairs. If there are any sagging or broken stems in the wicker, the repairs should be undertaken by a professional. In France, such artisans are easy to find, but that may not be the case once a piece has been shipped elsewhere.

Furniture with woodworm should always be avoided. Not only does it seriously weaken the furniture, it can spread to other pieces in your home. If woodworm is discovered while shipping, it may be refused at customs and incur a hefty charge for destruction.

Wood veneer is not necessarily a sign of a more recent piece, or of lower quality. In the eighteenth century, a lot of finely crafted marquetry was created using wood veneer sections to create a pattern. While beautiful, it can be prone to lifting and cracking, often because the furniture has been kept in damp conditions. Veneer can be successfully repaired, but it is a job for an expert and raises the overall price of your purchase.

Sometimes, a piece of furniture may look surprisingly modern. There are "fashions" in home furnishings, and antiques are no exception. For centuries it was normal to buy armoires; they were typically one of a young bride's first pieces of furniture, used to store her linens and monogrammed sheets. Today, homes are used and decorated differently, and those same armoires are to be found lining the walls of many antique dealers' storage areas. Originally and traditionally made of solid walnut, cherry, or oak, they often undergo transformations as dealers try to follow trends, with paint finishes or even sand-blasting techniques used to transform the unwanted polishes.

An eighteenth-century chair with tapestry upholstery.

Caring for Antique Furniture

Antique furniture should improve with age, but this only holds true when pieces are well looked after. Wood, leather, and upholstery are all sensitive to their environment, and prevention of harm is always better than cure.

One of the easiest ways to damage antique wood is to place it in the wrong spot. Sunlight, heat, and damp are the three main culprits. Too much direct sun will fade and dry out the finish, while heat from radiators or fireplaces causes wood to expand and crack. Moisture, on the other hand, can make joints swell or veneer peel away.

Aim for somewhere with a consistent temperature and decent ventilation—nothing too hot, too cold, or too humid. If the heating is on in winter, keep it low overnight to avoid sudden temperature drops. If you need to store a piece for a while, avoid basements or attics; these rarely have steady conditions. If—in spite of all your precautions—your furniture does start to warp or split, try to catch the problem early. Seeking prompt advice from a professional restorer can help to prevent minor damage from escalating into something costly or irreparable.

Dust furniture regularly with a soft, dry cloth (avoid damp cloths or modern spray products, which can degrade old finishes). Once or twice a year, polish wood with natural beeswax or a specialist antique wax. Apply with one cloth, then buff using another clean, dry one. For faded wood, a colored wax can help restore a more uniform tone, but always test new products on a discreet patch first, just in case the finish doesn't react well. If you suddenly notice tiny holes in your furniture, you might be dealing with an insect infestation. It's best to act quickly: contact a professional restorer right away to prevent the issue spreading to other pieces.

ABOVE, LEFT
Late eighteenth-century country-style display dressers.

ABOVE, RIGHT
Chairs and paintings on sale at a professional fair in Avignon.

FACING PAGE
An eighteenth-century Austrian baroque writing desk with drawers, in wood painted with a faux-wood marquetry design.

FACING PAGE
Renovated antique tables, stools, and armoires are carefully positioned for best effect.

ABOVE, LEFT
Carved wooden details on old armoires take on a different mood with a coat of paint.

ABOVE, RIGHT
When painting a carved wooden door, use a lighter color to highlight details.

PAGES 184 AND 185
At Chez Nous Campagne, simple antique furniture is restored, refurbished, and adapted to suit contemporary interiors.

PAGES 186–187
At Balines in Normandy, a dozen antique and *brocante* dealers are grouped together in a shared selling space.

If a drawer begins to stick, try rubbing a little candle wax or natural furniture wax along the edges to ease the slide. For dry or cracked leather desktops, a small amount of beeswax or neutral leather cream can restore suppleness, but always spot-test first to check the result. Colored leather tops tend to fade over time and can also benefit from a neutral-colored shoe cream or leather cream.

Damage can be caused by dragging furniture while moving it. It's always a good idea to move heavy pieces using two people, supporting the weight from underneath where construction is sturdiest. Be careful not to lift chairs from the top rail they can easily come apart. Tables with fold-out leaves also need careful handling. Lift from their frame or legs, not by the top, to avoid harming the intricate construction beneath.

Restoring antique furniture is about striking a balance: the aim should be to preserve as much of the original as possible, while ensuring the piece is structurally sound and ready for use. It's best to leave extensive restoration to a qualified professional—they'll ensure traditional materials and techniques are used, rather than modern shortcuts that can undermine the piece's integrity and long-term value.

For minor home repairs, proceed with care. If a veneer is chipped or lifting, attend to the problem as soon as possible—small pieces go missing easily, and finding matching veneers is notoriously tricky. Delicate fragments of wood or veneer can be held down with masking tape (never adhesive tape) until professionally repaired. For small fixes, use water-soluble wood glue rather than superglue.

Finally, you might want to insure particularly rare pieces, in which case a professional valuation can be extremely helpful. You will gain a better understanding not only of your collection's current worth, but also how that might change over time, ensuring accurate coverage both now and in the future.

MEET THE EXPERT

Cécile Schmitt

Chez Nous Campagne
Bubertré, Normandy
chez-nous-campagne.com
@chez_nous_campagne

In a quiet green valley in Normandy, a seventeenth-century presbytery, flanked by a few weathered barns, is home to the company Chez Nous Campagne. The quiet exterior belies the hive of activity within, hidden behind the thick stone walls.

Constantly on the hunt for simple, country-style furniture, Cécile and her team bring each find back to the atelier, where it is cleaned and restored by hand before being offered for sale. From farm tables and cupboards, to chairs and chests of drawers, every piece is individually appraised before restoration begins. While some items are sanded and painted, others need only a simple clean and polish—whatever is required to make them suitable for a modern setting.

Furniture is turned around quickly, and each weekend a loyal local community flocks to the on-site boutique and tearoom. The shop, housed in a large, converted barn, is styled with an eye for warmth and familiarity, blending antique finds with contemporary ceramics and textiles from selected designers.

Although much of the stock is available online, it is well worth paying a visit in person. Guests can linger in the adjoining tearoom; once a painter's studio, it overlooks the garden and is bathed in natural light. Each year, the space is refreshed by a contemporary artist, who reimagines the setting anew.

CÉCILE'S TIPS

Let patina speak. Not every piece needs to be repainted—sometimes a good scrub and a coat of wax are all it takes to restore its beauty.

CHAPTER 10

Architectural and Garden Antiques

Pallets holding carved stone fragments and an iron pergola canopy vie for attention with decorative garden gates.

On their first visit to an antique dealer specializing in architectural elements, the uninitiated buyer would be forgiven for wondering where the stock comes from. It is surprising to see crates piled high with reclaimed floor tiles, or barns lined with expertly painted wood paneling. However, many people don't realize that these items are actually part of a circular economy that in many ways preserves the craftsmanship of another era.

Inheriting a château is no small affair, and not every historic property ends up in the hands of someone willing, or able, to care for it. Famously, one château in Normandy lost its entire interior after a former owner gambled it away. Across France, many grand homes still stand silent and shuttered, abandoned for years, even decades. During this limbo period, they're often vulnerable to being stripped bare. I've come across many such places in France, emptied of their character long before they pass into more careful hands. Fireplace mantels, iron railings, carved doors, and marble sinks—some of the most distinctive features—can quietly vanish, sold off before restoration ever begins. It's an uncomfortable truth, but one that has fueled a particular kind of market: the trade in architectural and garden antiques.

Moreover, despite growing efforts to protect architectural heritage, there are still moments when a property is refurbished with little regard for its original features, and the existing parquet floors, paving stones, and even wooden paneling for entire rooms can end up on the antique market.

Yet not all salvage is born of neglect. In many ways, it is a poetic form of preservation. While some old homes are dismantled, others are simply beyond repair, but their parts can be rescued, reused by respectful renovators, or reimagined in new settings. A former pair of window shutters might be used indoors as closet doors in a guest room. Old tiles can be reinstalled in small spaces like powder rooms or entryways, making a strong design statement. Even a simple stone corbel, mounted on the wall, can hold a candle or small artwork, adding architectural rhythm to a room.

We don't usually think of antiques in the garden, but they lend themselves beautifully to outdoor settings. Weathered urns, moss-covered stone pillars, carved lintels, and rusted iron gates: these objects are a soulful way to bring beauty, depth, and atmosphere to an outdoor space. Seating might come in the form of a cast-iron bench or a repurposed stone slab—items often found at local fairs and markets—placed alongside mismatched terra-cotta pots, or stone troughs reimagined as sculptural planters.

However you use your antiques, the key is balance. These old pieces need space to breathe. Rather than crowding a space with multiple architectural elements, let just one or two speak, surrounding them with simpler forms and natural materials that allow their character to shine without overwhelming the scene.

ABOVE, LEFT
Antique plates displayed beneath a vintage iron garden chair.

ABOVE, RIGHT
An antique workbench serves as a console and support for a large bird cage and iron planters.

FACING PAGE
A stone statue is juxtaposed with ornate picture frames, artisan ceramics, and a sturdy wooden table.

Period Materials and Decorative Features

France's architectural heritage is incredibly rich, and each region has its own vocabulary of materials and motifs. In Normandy, you're likely to come across weathered oak beams, pale limestone lintels, and decorative ironwork with ecclesiastical origins. Further south, in Provence, you'll find yourself surrounded by terra-cotta tiles, shuttered wooden window frames, and sun-bleached stone pillars.

Whether found in a village *brocante* or sourced through a trusted dealer, these elements have a timeless quality and are endlessly adaptable. Although these pieces weren't made for today's homes, with a bit of imagination they can enhance even the most modern houses and gardens.

FACING PAGE
After some careful repair, these large entrance doors with ironwork will be perfect to embellish a building façade.

ABOVE, LEFT
Weathered stone baskets of plenty make a statement in any garden.

ABOVE, RIGHT
The monumental head of a statue looks displeased to be left waiting among obelisks and other stone details.

Stone elements

Stone items can be found in every possible shape and size at antique fairs and dealers' premises. It's not unusual to come across statues, benches, carved spheres, urns, decorative finials, or fragments of balustrade. On some occasions—through highly specialized dealers—you may discover entire garden walls salvaged from a château, complete with pillars and iron gates still bolted in place.

Fountains, old drinking troughs, and sinks are more common, though; often carved from limestone or marble, they are ideal for repurposing as water features. Some arrive intact, others need a little imagination and plumbing. Stone steps might be sold singly or as part of a larger staircase, but they require precise measurements—there is little margin for error when it comes to stone.

Ironwork

Antique ironwork requires close inspection. Surface rust is to be expected, but deeper corrosion can weaken key joints or scrollwork beyond repair. Still, there is much that is worth salvaging: railings and gates with ornate flourishes, balcony guards, seating, or eye-catching architectural braces and brackets. Old greenhouse frames can sometimes be found, with or without glass. With the right care and expertise, they can be restored to their original function, or appreciated simply for their sculptural form.

Zinc objects

Used for the famous oeil-de-boeuf window frame and for decorative trim along roof lines, zinc is a material that ages well, even after a hundred years or more. In addition to architectural elements, you'll often find zinc repurposed in the garden in the form of watering cans, planters, and washtubs, many of which are still perfectly functional, while others simply display a beautiful patina.

Roof tiles

There are dealers who specialize almost entirely in roofing materials, and for good reason. The regional differences in French roofing are quite distinctive. In the north, there are several kinds of traditional roof tiles, most notably the dark gray slate associated with the Paris skyline. These tiles are easy to find in good condition and can last well over a century if properly installed.

ABOVE, LEFT
A pair of iron gates with a mail slot.

ABOVE, RIGHT
Early nineteenth-century zinc oeil-de-boeuf window surrounds, which were originally positioned on rooftops.

Flat clay tiles, or *tuiles plates*, are also common; their uneven, weathered surfaces grow more beautiful with time—although more fragile, too. From the nineteenth century onward, these were replaced by larger, interlocking tiles known as *tuiles mécaniques*. Sturdier and more uniform, they are easier to lay, while still retaining the warmth of traditional clay. In the south of France, the roofs are traditionally clad in curved half-tube-shaped tiles, inextricably linked to the identity of Provence today.

Floor tiles

Floor tiles can also be found in abundance, but rarely in consistent quantities. They range from eighteenth-century terra-cotta to vividly patterned cement tiles from the nineteenth century. If you are lucky, they will only need dusting off and washing with a good quality soap, but sometimes they'll arrive with a layer of cement stuck to the back. These require patient chipping and cleaning before reuse.

Garden furniture

Antique garden furniture is guaranteed to add a special charm to any outdoor space, whether it be a bench with cast-iron legs supporting simple wooden slats, or swirls of ironwork with multiple coats of paint that reveal changing fashions. Chipped paint adds patina, but if preferred it can be sandblasted back to the metal and protected with an invisible seal. As well as tables and seating, look out for large iron lamps that can be suspended from walls or placed on supports for additional lighting in the garden.

ABOVE, LEFT
Clay roof tiles can be sourced easily, although it is important to respect regional styles.

ABOVE, RIGHT
Refurbished vintage garden furniture never loses its charm.

Pots and planters

Old terra-cotta pots can be found at antique fairs and stores everywhere. Prior to the widespread use of plastic planters, nurseries raised their plants in beautiful handmade terra-cotta flowerpots; provided they are treated with respect, they can serve for decades. You might come across large earthenware pots with cracks that have been repaired using large metal staples; don't be put off: they are sturdy, and their repair showcases a long-forgotten savoir faire. Medici urns are another popular style, and their vase-like shape and ornamentation impart a touch of elegance to any garden.

Fireplaces

Fireplace surrounds in stone or marble appear regularly at markets. A well-balanced stone surround is a great find; it is one of the most adaptable architectural features and can usually be transported without major problems. Marble versions can be tempting, but they require greater caution: marble is fragile and breaks easily when handled.

Wooden flooring and paneling

Antique wooden floorboards are rarely uniform and can be tricky to align, but the results are highly rewarding. Specialized dealers should have a choice of design—from parquet and chevron to wide rustic planks, which can be adapted to most surface areas—and they can offer advice on installation and maintenance. Some dealers also carry wooden wall paneling, either as individual loose panels or, more rarely, sufficient paneling to line an entire room. Often made from oak, walnut, or chestnut, paneling was originally designed to insulate rooms and can still serve that purpose today. Condition varies widely, however, and pieces are typically graded by wear and completeness. Dealers may propose reclaimed paneling, with or without original detailing, leaving installation and finishing to the buyer's discretion.

ABOVE, LEFT
Carved stone fire surrounds can be adapted to existing fireplaces.

ABOVE, RIGHT
Large Anduze pots are timeless and can be displayed indoors or outdoors.

FACING PAGE
Long sections of gilded wooden paneling are presented unceremoniously on the ground at the professional fair in Perpignan.

PAGE 198
A nineteenth-century frame with carved wooden details awaits a new mirror.

PAGE 199
The beauty of the original blue-gray paint finish is heightened by the patina of age.

MEET THE EXPERT

Arnaud de Saint-Martin

Bellême, Normandy
@arnauddesaintmartin

Tucked away in Nogent-le-Rotrou, a medieval city and former capital of the Perche region in northwest France, Arnaud's atelier is housed in an abandoned factory. A well-known figure in the world of architectural salvage, Arnaud specializes in antique doors and wood paneling sourced from homes and châteaux across France. Although it may be surprising to some, his wares do not come polished, dusted, or even cleaned—they come as they are, with their honorable marks of age.

His constantly changing stock is stored in the old glass-roofed warehouse, bathed in a soft light, but there's no staged perfection here, just quiet order. A thousand or so doors are stacked and sorted by type, each one carefully marked on the inside edge for easy retrieval, with measurements, age, and notes on provenance.

Much of Arnaud's business comes from interior designers, although private clients from around the world also get in touch with their wish lists, either making an appointment to visit or working with Arnaud remotely. With a background in property renovation and historic restoration, Arnaud is well placed to advise on suitable styles and can offer made-to-measure adaptations when possible.

ARNAUD'S TIPS:

"It's all about connections," he states. If you build trust with dealers, their network will start working for you. "Everyone knows what I'm looking for," he confides. "Sometimes people just turn up with a couple of doors on a trailer, or call me to collect some quickly from a building site."

The Collector's Eye

When paying a visit to a specialist in architectural salvage, you may well find yourself out in a courtyard or field, facing the elements. By their very nature, many of these items were created to be used outdoors and naturally remain there, weathering rain and sun without any fuss. Their scale also makes them easier to stock in a field than in a chic boutique. In these settings it's important to take your time—and watch your step! You don't want to trip over an errant section of railing or stone finial. Have a tape measure in your pocket, and if you're searching for something specific, take photos and notes as you go.

Provenance is especially interesting when searching for architectural elements. Dealers who specialize in these antiques—such as those at L'Isle-sur-la-Sorgue or the Puces de Saint-Ouen near Paris—can often tell you where a piece was salvaged, and sometimes even the building from which it was taken. This context can add both emotional and historical value to a find.

However, architectural salvage is as much about intuition as it is about knowledge. While larger fairs attract professional dealers, it could be at a village *brocante* or weekend *vide-grenier* that you stumble upon a hidden gem. Early morning visits are best, especially in the warmer months, and it helps to arrive with gardening gloves, along with something for taking notes. Be prepared to dig through piles of unwieldy items, and look past dirt or rust to see a piece's potential.

It's also essential to consider the practicalities of a purchase. Make sure you have the measurements of your space to hand, and measure the piece you're interested in twice, to avoid calculation errors. You'll also need to think about weight—stone troughs, marble basins, and cast-iron fountains can be incredibly heavy and may require reinforced foundations or heavy machinery for installation.

Some French dealers offer shipping for individual pieces, but this can be costly and slow. If you're buying multiple pieces, it may be worth arranging a consolidated shipment or working with a broker who specializes in international freight for antiques.

Lastly, while surface wear and natural patina are desirable, serious damage is not. For wood, check for signs of active woodworm: tiny fresh holes or dusty residue. For stone features, avoid structural cracks or fissures that could compromise the integrity of the piece once exposed to changing temperatures. With iron, some surface rust is to be expected and can be treated, but if there is deep pitting or flaking, this may impact the object's durability. Over time, severe corrosion can cause structural damage, so you might want to think twice before purchasing.

At the Puces de Saint-Ouen, majestic iron gates that once graced the walls of the arsenal at Cherbourg now await a new home to protect.

Caring for Architectural and Garden Antiques

Once your architectural salvage or garden object has been installed, its maintenance becomes a long-term commitment. Antique items have already withstood decades, if not centuries, of use, but they still need thoughtful care to endure in modern environments. Over time, well-chosen pieces will only become more beautiful, settling into their surroundings and imbuing your home with history.

In general, older materials benefit from gentle handling and seasonal attention. Avoid modern chemical cleaners, which can strip away decades of natural patina. Stone—especially limestone and sandstone—is best cleaned with a soft-bristled brush and water. Do not use high-pressure jets or acidic cleaners, which can erode the surface.

Terra-cotta is porous and prone to cracking in frost. If left outside year-round, pots and tiles should be lifted slightly off the ground to promote drainage and air circulation. Rather than planting directly into antique pots, use pot liners to help preserve the originals' structural integrity. If a white residue—a buildup of calcium—appears on the surface, gently wipe it away with a damp cloth and a solution of water and white vinegar. Avoid scrubbing too hard, as this can damage the original glaze or finish. For encaustic and cement tiles, clean with mild soap and water only, never bleach. Buffing with a natural wax polish can help restore surface sheen and add protection, but it should be used sparingly. Terra-cotta floor tiles should be washed regularly with a gentle soap, and occasionally treated with a coat of flaxseed oil, which feeds the clay and prevents it from becoming dull.

To clean and restore wooden pieces, start with a mild wood soap and a soft cloth. If needed, lightly sand the surface to remove grime, old varnish, or chipped paint, then treat with linseed oil, beeswax polish, or a breathable finish like shellac. Avoid polyurethane, which can seal in moisture and cause long-term damage. Wooden items used outdoors should be raised off the ground and, ideally, sheltered from the elements. If you plan to repaint any features, opt for a breathable mineral-based or limewash paint, in keeping with traditional finishes.

Wrought- and cast-iron can be treated by brushing off loose rust, applying a rust converter, then sealing with iron oxide primer and outdoor metal paint. Zinc, on the other hand, naturally develops an attractive soft gray-blue patina. To care for it, rinse occasionally with water and a soft cloth. Avoid abrasives or acidic cleaners, and line zinc planters to prevent corrosion from soil.

Copper similarly develops a distinctive patina—a characteristic green known as verdigris. To return it to its original finish, clean with a mix of lemon juice and salt, or apply a dedicated copper cleaner. Let it sit, then buff gently with a soft cloth. If you prefer its aged look, simply allow the verdigris to develop naturally. Copper's patina is a protective layer, as well as a visual asset.

FACING PAGE
Whenever possible, try to preserve the original glass in old doors.

PAGE 204
A small cast-iron table is refitted with a new wooden plateau.

PAGE 205
In the best tradition of antique dealers, Florence creates spectacular displays with an eclectic mix of her current stock.

PAGES 206–207
Antique dealer Un Singe en Hiver, at the Puces de Saint-Ouen, specializes in outsized products.

MEET THE EXPERT

Florence de Boissieu

Brocante de La Bruyère
Rungis, Île-de-France
brocantedelabruyere.com
@brocantedelabruyere

For nearly two decades, Florence de Boissieu has been sourcing an ever-evolving mix of antique armoires, mirrors, tableware, and outdoor accessories for her boutique, Brocante de La Bruyère. A seasoned *brocanteuse*, she built a loyal following from her countryside barn, showing at regional fairs and welcoming clients from across France and beyond.

Her operation shifted, however, when her husband took over a wholesale plant business at Rungis, the sprawling food and flower market just outside Paris. With access to two expansive glass warehouses, Florence saw the chance to open up her collection to a new, professional clientele. While antiques aren't typically part of the Rungis offering, the setting proved ideal.

Florence's stock remains broad, but her garden furniture and décor are particular standouts: stone statuary, tool benches, terra-cotta pots, cast-iron planters, and zinc bathtubs. With room to create generous vignettes, she sets the scene beautifully, making it easy for designers and florists to snap up striking items before or after their flower runs.

Although Rungis is only open to trade buyers, Florence also sells online and regularly shares her latest finds on Instagram.

FLORENCE'S TIPS

Don't be afraid to use objects in an unexpected way. Weathered teapots or zinc troughs make excellent pots and planters.

Fairs and Markets

Whether it's a small country fair or a large international gathering, antique markets and *brocantes* are the most practical way of seeing a large choice of objects in one spot. For antiquing enthusiasts, weekly markets promise a day of varied activity, from browsing wares to sampling local delicacies, while for seasoned treasure hunters annual fairs offer the opportunity to make big sweeps and pick up great finds by the vanload.

Both big cities and small country villages hold local and annual events, so it's always worth checking what is on if you are planning to visit. There are several online websites that list fairs by date and by region, which are regularly updated with the latest information. We particularly recommend **brocabrac.fr** and **vide-greniers.org**. Both websites allow you to search for professional and pop-up events by town name or zip code.

Paris and Suburbs

Scattered along sidewalks, on makeshift tables, under white temporary tents, or directly on the ground, you'll find a mix of professional and private sellers popping up all over Paris. Be aware, however, that among these Parisian vendors, some are more reliable than others.

Place des Vosges

75003/75004 Paris

Occasionally, special events, such as the Brocante du Marais, are organized at Place des Vosges. These antique markets typically occur once or twice a year—often in September and the spring— with white tents run by professional sellers lining the square and extending toward the Village Saint- Paul. Displaying a wide array of fine antiques, as well as vintage items, the location also offers easy access to the neighborhood's art galleries and the nearby Saint-Paul district for further exploration.

FACING PAGE
Every Saturday morning, the fair at Villeneuve-lès-Avignon welcomes antique enthusiasts from around the world.

PAGE 211
Two outsized terra-cotta medici urns dwarf a charming armchair upholstered in toile de Jouy fabric.

République

Place de la République, 75003/75010 Paris

Though not a weekly market, Place de la République and its surrounding streets—such as Rue Beaurepaire, leading up to Canal Saint-Martin, and Boulevard du Temple, heading toward Bastille—regularly host *brocantes* and antique fairs. These markets offer a real mix, from bric-a-brac and vintage household items to finer antiques curated by professionals. Expect everything from twentieth-century furniture and collectible art to secondhand designer clothing. Dates and exact locations of these markets can be found on vide-greniers.org, often under the category "Premium Events."

Bouquinistes

Quais de la Seine, 75004 Paris

Stretching along the Seine river, the legendary green book stalls—fixtures of the Parisian landscape since the sixteenth century—offer a trove of vintage and antique books, posters, prints, and collectibles. While many stalls specialize in French poetry, literature, or travel, a few are run by art enthusiasts, with curations ranging from rare editions and engravings to vintage photographs and contemporary paintings.

Undesignable Market

32 Rue des Fossés Saint-Bernard, 75005 Paris

Lining the entrance to the Sorbonne's Pierre and Marie Curie building, this *brocante*-cum-antique market focuses on twentieth-century art and design. Launched in 2015, the collective of professional sellers specializes in vintage French, Italian, German, Scandinavian, and Dutch furniture, lighting, and décor. It's especially strong on mid-century, postmodern, and retro 1970s and '80s pieces, with plenty of named designers in the mix. Prices are higher than your average Paris flea market, but the curation is sharp, deals can be found, and sellers are open to negotiation. Held several times a year—usually in March, June, and September—from 6:30 a.m. to 6 p.m., exact dates of upcoming fairs are regularly updated on their website (undesignable.eu/en).

Saint-Sulpice

Place Saint-Sulpice, 75006 Paris

Spanning several weeks from May to June each year, themed fairs set up shop in front of the Saint- Sulpice church in the 6th arrondissement. Notable among them are the Salon des Antiquaires, which showcases a diverse range of furniture and art objects from the seventeenth to the twentieth centuries, including jewelry, textiles, vintage fashion, and fine art pieces, and the Salon de la Bibliophilie, which focuses on rare and collectible books, manuscripts, and prints.

Puces de Vanves

Avenue Georges Lafenestre, 75014 Paris

Located in the 14th arrondissement of Paris, this is one of the most dependable and accessible antique markets in the city. Every Saturday and Sunday morning—come rain or shine—vendors line the street, offering a range of items from silverware and antique jewelry to artwork, rugs, small pieces of furniture, and other easy-to-carry treasures. While parking can be tricky, it is easily reached by métro, starting just steps from the Porte de Vanves exit. The atmosphere is friendly and relaxed, but don't arrive too late—at 12:30 vendors begin packing up their stands, to head home for lunch.

Village Suisse

78 Avenue de Suffren, 75015 Paris

Just a stone's throw from the Eiffel Tower, the Village Suisse is a permanent antique collective known for its quality, exceptional curation, and unique shopping experience. Established in 1920, the market now comprises one hundred and fifty antique dealers, whose storefronts brim with a diverse selection of antiques. It is a particularly good place to find furniture and art.

Brocante de Passy

5 Impasse des Carrières, 75016 Paris

Tucked away in a small cobblestone cul-de-sac off Rue de Passy, this permanent vintage and antiques warehouse carries a diverse range of items, including books, tableware, oil paintings, furniture, mirrors, and art deco jewelry, all displayed in a charmingly chaotic fashion.

Puces de Saint-Ouen

Rue des Rosiers, 93400 Saint-Ouen-sur-Seine

With more than seventeen hundred permanent dealers, the Puces de Saint-Ouen is the largest antique center in the world. Also known as the Puces de Clignancourt, it has existed for over one hundred and fifty years and is now divided into individual markets, each with its own particular style and atmosphere. The most iconic are Paul Bert and Vernaison, but the other markets deserve attention, too. Head to Jules Vallès for books and vintage fashion, Serpette for high-end antiques, or Biron for eighteenth- and nineteenth-century furniture. Additional boutiques line the connecting roads, and some dealers set up makeshift street stalls, so it is impossible to see the entire market in just one visit. Using a map of the markets, focus on just one or two, and save the others to enjoy on your next visit. It is only open from Friday to Monday, and vendors spend their weekdays replenishing and switching out their stock, in the hope of luring back loyal antique hunters the following weekend.

Village des Antiquaires, Versailles

13 Passage de la Geôle, 78000 Versailles

Not far from the château, this historic antique district has been a fixture in Versailles for nearly forty years. Home to around fifty expert dealers across four interconnected courtyards and alleys—once the city's first court and prison—it now houses galleries and shopfronts brimming with fine art, modern paintings, period furniture, antique jewelry, ceramics, and artisan workshops. Whether you're hunting for Louis XVI furniture, vintage fashion, silverware, rare books, or something modern but unique, a visit to these dealers is well worth the short train ride from Paris.

Foire de Chatou

Île des Impressionnistes, 78400 Chatou

Twice a year, in March and September, on a small island in the middle of the Seine, several hundred white tents are erected and readied for the antiquing event of the season. Vendors arrive from all over France and settle in for ten days of buying and selling, lunches with friends, and making contact with clients, both old and new. Originally known as the Foire à la Brocante et aux Jambons (Flea Market and Ham Fair)—and not short of good places to eat—it is divided into a grid of alleys and walkways centered around four large covered halls, and should be approached methodically by buyers. Shippers are on hand on the first and last day of the fair, and can be contacted in between for pickups.

North and East

Amiens: Réderie d'Amiens

Town center, 80000 Amiens

On two Sundays each year, in October and April, the city center of Amiens is given over to antiques. Up to two thousand vendors line over nine miles (15 km) of streets and attract tens of thousands of visitors. The official opening time is 5 a.m., but really keen buyers start their mornings at midnight, and continue buying throughout the day. Flashlight in hand, professional buyers can be seen, often on bicycles, rushing around the town in the dark, hoping to find treasures before the crowds arrive. To buy successfully here, it is worth arriving the day before to park your vehicle and check into a hotel. Warm clothes and comfortable footwear are a must, as you will be walking for miles, literally. Those aiming to purchase in large volumes should consider working with a shipper and having goods collected on the go. With good organization, a large truck, and a healthy budget, a whole house could be furnished in a day at this fair.

DICTIONAIRE
Tome IX.
DES-DIS
DICTIONAIRE
Tome IV.
Tome XXI.
MEDI-MES
DICTIONAIRE DES SCIENCES MÉDICALES.
Tome XX.
HAB-HEM
DICTIONAIRE DES SCIENCES MÉDICALES.
Tome XIV.
EXC-FEM
DICTIONAIRE
Tome V.
CHA-COL
DICTIONAIRE DES SCIENCES MÉDICALES.
Tome I.
AMP

Belfort: Marché aux Puces de Belfort

Place d'Armes, 90000 Belfort

Held on the first Sunday of the month, the Marché aux Puces de Belfort is the largest flea market in eastern France, drawing collectors, decorators, and antiquing enthusiasts alike. With over one hundred and fifty exhibitors, the market offers a diverse selection of antiques and vintage finds, but specializes in furniture, military memorabilia, twentieth-century prints, religious artifacts, and timepieces. The atmosphere is lively but not overwhelming, prices are often more reasonable than in Parisian markets, and parking in town is easy, making it a great place for a leisurely browse.

Lille: Braderie de Lille

City center, 59000 Lille

More than thirty miles (48 km) of streets are shut down for this monumental, biannual open-air event, held on the first weekend in September and the last in March. A joyous mix of antiques, food, beer, and general bazaar, it attracts ten thousand vendors and over two million visitors each year. Residents are also known to take part by setting up their own impromptu stands in front of their homes, selling everything from secondhand clothing to antique heirlooms. The trick is to identify the area selling antiques and stick to it. If you can, book into a hotel and get first dibs with some pre-dawn shopping. Although the market is officially open from Saturday morning to Sunday evening, some vendors start as early as Friday night.

Southeast

Carpentras

Parking des Platanes, Avenue Jean Jaurés, 84200 Carpentras

On Sundays, this large parking lot is devoted to an excellent weekly *brocante*, with vendors offering a diverse range of furniture, artwork, and Provençal homeware. Trading is not permitted before 9 a.m., so arriving early is only necessary if you want to grab a good parking spot. Although parking on site fills up fast, available spaces can normally be found a little way down the road, making it a convenient market for day visitors or those looking to purchase larger pieces.

Eygalières

Village center, 13810 Eygalières

On the last Sunday of the month, the charming Provençal village of Eygalières turns into a temporary *brocante*. Vendors line the main street, offering a variety of antiques and vintage items, while locals and tourists wander up and down, making purchases or simply soaking up the relaxed atmosphere. There's no rush to shop, and there are many cafés and restaurants in the village to take advantage of, making it a pleasant and leisurely outing. Although the market is small, it is appreciated for its picturesque setting and the unique treasures that can be found.

L'Isle-sur-la-Sorgue

Town center, 84000 L'Isle-sur-la-Sorgue

You'll discover more than just a market here: half of this small town is given over to antique and bric-a-brac stores. Considered by many to be the antiques mecca of the south of France, it is certainly not to be missed. Alongside the numerous boutiques, there are six permanent antique villages, gathering over three hundred dealers, open from Friday to Sunday, or by appointment. There is also a weekend street market, where vendors unpack their goods directly onto the sidewalk. The town can be somewhat confusing for first-time visitors, but if you proceed methodically it is a great place for secondhand finds. Parking spots fill up quickly, so it is advisable to arrive before 9 a.m. The town's large summer antique fair in mid-August—managed by the same organizers as the Foire de Chatou—is also worth the detour.

Lyon: Puces du Canal

5 Rue Eugène Pottier, 69100 Villeurbanne

One of France's largest and liveliest flea markets, the Puces du Canal unfolds weekly along the Jonage canal, on Thursday, Saturday, and Sunday. With over two hundred permanent stores and four hundred street vendors, it offers a vast selection at great prices. The market is divided into four distinct areas: Le Hangar, specializing in sixteenth- to twentieth-century pieces; La Halle Louis-la-Brocante, a maze of secondhand specialists; Le Village des Containers, focused on design and contemporary finds; and L'École, for upcycled, restored, and vintage goods. Besides shopping, there are seven on-site restaurants to refuel on traditional Lyon-style dishes. The market is easily accessible via Lyon's métro system, and parking— albeit limited—is available nearby.

Nice

Le Cours Saleya, 06300 Nice

A stone's throw from the seafront in Nice, the pedestrian-only Cours Saleya hosts a popular food and flower market during the week. Every Monday, however, the area transforms into a lively antique fair and flea market, offering everything from vintage jewelry to old books. The Mediterranean setting provides a lovely backdrop for browsing this vibrant market.

Villeneuve-lès-Avignon

Place Charles David, 30400 Villeneuve-lès-Avignon

Every Saturday morning, a hundred or so secondhand vendors set up their stands and offer their wares to an appreciative crowd of tourists and locals. The market is particularly known for its excellent selection of paintings, textiles, ceramics, and Provençal earthenware. Parking is easy, so after browsing the market, take the time to explore the town on foot and enjoy a leisurely lunch at one of the nearby cafés and bistros.

Southwest

Bordeaux

Place des Quinconces, 33000 Bordeaux

Twice a year, in April and November, more than two hundred vendors settle in for the long haul: two weeks of nonstop trading. The event's size draws visitors from near and far, eager to explore a broad selection of antiques and collectibles. Stands and displays are refreshed daily with new items, and during the spring edition there is the added charm of a botanical fair alongside the *brocante*.

Toulouse: Brocante des Allées

Allées Forain-François Verdier, 31000 Toulouse

For over forty years, this monthly fair has taken place in the center of Toulouse on the first weekend of the month. With more than one hundred vendors selling a mix of antiques, vintage furniture, and art, it is as much a favorite with locals as it is with visitors.

Déballages

The term *déballages* (which literally means "clearings") refers to fairs that are, in principle, reserved for professionals. These no-frills events take place monthly or bimonthly across France and follow a set circuit: from Béziers to Avignon, Montpellier, and Toulouse, then north to Chartres, Le Mans, and Compiègne. The fairs are typically scheduled on consecutive dates, making it possible for buyers to follow the whole route in one trip.

Entry requirements vary depending on the organizer. A French antique dealer will usually need to present official company paperwork to obtain an annual pass. For international buyers, the pass itself isn't always mandatory, but proper documentation proving professional status is still essential. While Chartres and Le Mans are known for their strict enforcement of paperwork requirements, entry to the fairs in the south of France can be more relaxed.

These fairs operate at a brisk pace. Gates open at 8 a.m. sharp—no transactions are permitted before then—and by 1 p.m., it's all wrapped up. There's little emphasis on display—this is about swift, no-nonsense dealings between seasoned traders who can assess pieces on the fly and make confident decisions in the moment.

The atmosphere is not conducive to lingering. Hesitation often means losing out, and competition is palpable. One important thing to remember is that these fairs are in more remote spots, so if you intend to purchase, be sure to have transportation available to collect immediately. The most prepared buyers arrive with a truck or are accompanied by a trusted shipper, ready to load as they go. In that case, clear paperwork becomes vital. Logistics are tight, and errors are not easily undone once the next fair is already underway.

But, it has to be said, there's something exhilarating about the pace of it all. If you get the opportunity to visit, it's worth experiencing a *déballage* at least once—even just to watch the fast exchange of decisions and quiet nods between those in the know.

For the latest fair dates and up-to-date practical information, visit **deballagesmarchands.fr**

Avignon: *Parc des Expositions, Route de Marseille, 84000*
Béziers: *Parc des Expositions, Route de Bédarieux, 34500*
Chartres: *CHARTREXPO, Avenue Jean Mermoz, 28000*
Le Mans: *Parc des Expositions, 1 Avenue du Parc des Expositions, 72000*
Margny-lès-Compiègne: *Pôle Événementiel Le Tigre, 2 Rue Jean Mermoz, 60280*
Montpellier/Pérols: *Parc des Expositions, Route de la Foire, 34470 Pérols*
Toulouse: *Le Grand Marché, 200 Avenue des Etats-Unis, 31200*

PAGE 212
At the fair at Villeneuve-lès-Avignon, antique books are displayed alongside small nineteenth-century paintings.

FACING PAGE
A frequent vendor at the Puces de Vanves, Yves Bourdon carefully attaches his largest tapestries to the street railings.

Auctions

Buying and bidding online has become routine, following eBay's domination of the market. But don't be mistaken—bidding on a live auction, where you can watch the auctioneer work the room, is a far more engaging experience.

A live auction house (*salle des ventes*, in French) is akin to theater. The auctioneer is the star of the show, and buyers are simultaneously audience and actors. A good auctioneer knows their products and their public, and loves to cajole, encouraging potential buyers to sneak in a higher bid to get one step closer to acquiring the coveted item.

If you are in France and have the opportunity to visit an auction house and a sale, don't hesitate. For those intending to purchase, make the most of the viewing opportunities to inspect the objects before the sale starts. Most auctions provide online or physical catalogs and publicly display items in the days leading up to the sale. Take your time to peruse, make notes, jot down lot numbers, take photos, and, once home or back at your hotel, take a moment to research the artist, the brand, or any details you can find about the objects that have caught your eye. There is nothing worse than scoring at auction, only to realize afterward that the purchase is less valuable than you thought. Information is power, and the more you know about the items for sale, the more you will enjoy the event.

I once had the pleasure of clearing out a sale while buying on behalf of a client. We had looked at all the items carefully before the sale started, and I attended the auction in person. With her generous budget—and a huge amount of luck—we were the only serious bidders in the room. While a few local antique dealers started bidding against us, they soon realized that we were buying with intent. Some left us to it, while a couple sat back to enjoy the show.

Drouot: A French Institution

9 Rue Drouot, 75009 Paris

Founded in 1852, Drouot is France's oldest auction house and the seat of the capital's Chamber of Auctioneers. With sixteen auction rooms hosting public and private sales from over sixty independent auction houses, it has long been a hub for buyers and sellers, both local and international. Some three thousand visitors pass through its doors daily, whether to bid, browse, or simply experience the energy of a live auction.

Housed in an impressive glass building, the sixteen auction rooms are split between three floors. Upstairs, you'll find gallery-like auction rooms where visitors can browse lots prior to auction. Some sales group items by theme, while others are mixed estate clearances, but Drouot is particularly known for art, fine jewelry, luxury fashion, antique furniture, and tapestries. Interested buyers often make themselves known to the auction staff in advance, signaling their intent by examining items before the sale. Their names are noted to ensure that the auctioneers are aware of key bidders.

In the basement—where a second set of auction rooms is located—the atmosphere is notably heated and crowded. This is where the live auctions take place. Each room is set up much like a courtroom. An auctioneer and their team preside from a raised dais, faced by rows of bidders seated in folding chairs. Auxiliary staff move lots back and forth, and a standing audience watches from behind the seated bidders. Agents for phone bids are seated along the room's edge.

Auctions proceed by lot number, so buyers come prepared with a list of lots in numerical order. A raised hand is enough to bid—there are no paddles here. The bidders remain quiet, leaving all the drama to the auctioneer. If successful, the buyer receives a slip of paper with their lot details to collect their purchase or organize shipping. While some attendees stay to observe for a while, others bid promptly and leave, either moving on to another room or having come for a specific item only.

Some sales are brisk, building anticipation quickly, while others take on a more leisurely pace. Estimates may be wildly off or surprisingly accurate—artworks priced at €100–€200 can easily reach €800, while fashion items like YSL and Celine bags often fall below their estimates, sometimes selling for as little as €300.

Although the proceedings are conducted in French, you don't need to be fluent to follow along. The current bid, lot number, and photograph of the item are displayed on an overhead screen, making it easy for everyone to track the auction.

Other Auction Houses

If you plan to visit Paris specifically to experience live auctions, you'd be remiss not to explore some of the city's other renowned auction houses. For high-end sales, featuring objects of significant value, it is best to be accompanied by an agent who will bid on your behalf and consult with you before raising the price. For smaller stakes, register for the sale and enjoy.

Sotheby's

83 Rue du Faubourg Saint-Honoré, 75008 Paris

Famous for its fine furniture and decorative art auctions, Sotheby's is particularly known for hosting collections from celebrated figures. Past auctions include the sale of Karl Lagerfeld's personal items, as well as other luxury lots such as fine wines, cars, and high-end fashion.

Christie's

9 Rue Matignon, 75008 Paris

Housed in a mansion near the Avenue des Champs-Élysées, Christie's France offers a refined auction experience with seven showrooms and two auction rooms. Sales take place both on-site and online, covering gold, jewelry, contemporary paintings, manuscripts, furniture, and objets d'art. Collectors and artists can also have works appraised by the auction house's experts.

Bonhams

6 Avenue Hoche, 75008 Paris

Bonhams adds a global dimension to the Paris auction scene, offering sales in fine art, watches, and classic cars in a central Paris location. With an eclectic mix of categories, it attracts collectors with diverse interests hoping to find a rare gem.

Digard

17 Rue Drouot, 75009 Paris

With a strong reputation in the art world, Digard specializes in high-end sales, focusing on both emerging artists and household names, such as Jean Dufy and Josef Albers. The house also offers luxury collectibles, attracting buyers seeking unique and dynamic pieces.

Millon

19 Rue de la Grange Batelière, 75009 Paris

Practically next door to Drouot, Millon is known for its trade in Asian and modern European art, rare books, and high-end jewelry. It has a long history of presenting underappreciated works that later gain major recognition.

Aguttes

164 bis Avenue Charles-de-Gaulle, 92200 Neuilly-sur-Seine

Established in 1974, Aguttes is a family-owned auction house and is one of the largest in Europe today. Focused on high-end art and unique collectibles, with a special division for musical instruments, it attracts a strong international clientele to Paris's western suburb.

Country Auctions

While the larger auction houses in Paris may feel intimidating, French towns regularly have their own auctioneer, and propose sales on preannounced themes throughout the year. Beloved by locals, these auctions often have allotted seats at the front of the room for regular clients, who engage in chitchat with the auctioneer as the sale progresses.

Online Auctions

If you can't attend in person, you can still follow the action online, and even take part. Simply create an account on your preferred auction house website and you'll be able to bid on live auctions or on exclusive online sales. Just make sure to fix your upper spending limit and note down the commission rate on your items to avoid any shocks to your bank account.

Interencheres.com

A favorite for online bidding, this site offers everything from fine art and antiques to design pieces and collectibles. Detailed catalogs are available before most sales, so you can research and refine your selection in advance.

Address Book

Dealers and Shops

Bordeaux

Au Temple de la Chine
15 Place Canteloup
33800 Bordeaux
Group of dealers; various specialties
lesbrocanteursdupassage.fr

Village Notre Dame
61–67 Rue Notre Dame
33000 Bordeaux
Group of dealers; various specialties
@villagenotredame

Burgundy

Galerie Rouget de Lisle
14 Rue de la République
21340 Nolay
Antique paintings
@galerie_antiquites_rdl

Village des Antiquaires
21 Boulevard Saint-Jacques
21200 Beaune
Group of dealers; various specialties
Facebook: Le Village des Antiquaires Beaune

Champagne

Reassort & Couverts
(Maurice and Patricia di Matteo, see p. 58)
Showroom: Champagne
(by appointment only)
Online store and stand at fairs in Paris
Silver flatware
@reassortcouverts
ebay.fr/str/reassortcouvert

Côte d'Azur

Maison Pampille
10 Rue Droite
06300 Nice
Antique furniture
@maison_pampille

Lille

Saint André Antiquités
22 Avenue du Maréchal de Lattre de Tassigny
59350 Saint-André-lez-Lille
Group of dealers; various specialties
Facebook: Antiquités le village

Loire

BCA Matériaux Anciens
Route de Craon – l'Hôtellerie-de-Flée
49500 Segré-en-Anjou Bleu
Architectural antiques
bca-antiquematerials.com
@bcamateriauxanciens

Normandy

L'Armillaire Ancienne
(Marc Razé, see p. 49)
Showroom: 27000 Évreux
(by appointment only)
Online store and stands at various fairs including Foire de Chatou (see p. 229)
Books and illustrations
armillaireancienne.com/en/
@armillaireancienne_oldbooks

Sophie and Marc Boutfol
Showroom: 50360 Beuzeville-la-Bastille
(by appointment only)
Stand at Foire de Chatou
Eighteenth-century objects
@boutfolsophie

Brocante de Balines
Route Nationale 12
27130 Verneuil-sur-Avre
Group of dealers; various specialties
@brocantedebalines

Chez Nous Campagne
(Cécile Schmitt, see p. 184)
Les Joncherets
61190 Bubertré
Brocante objects
chez-nous-campagne.com
@chez_nous_campagne

Cyril Fassier
20 Place de l'Hotel de Ville
61290 Longny-au-Perche
Brocante objects
@antiquites_fassier

FACING PAGE
At the Puces de Saint-Ouen, a Louis XVI-style sofa in red velvet creates an effective counterpoint.

PAGES 222–223
Regular dealers at the Foire de Chatou gather together for lunch on makeshift tables.

Galerie de l'Astrée
8 Rue Damiette
76000 Rouen
High-end antiques
@galeriedelastree.argeades

Galerie du Crabe
(Yves Berger, see p. 33)
22 Rue du Dr Letourneur
50400 Granville
Antique paintings, engravings, and books
@lecrabedegranville

Harmonie du Logis
Domaine d'Avoise
61250 Radon
and
1256 Route de Pont l'Évêque,
14800 Bonneville-sur-Touques
Architectural antiques
harmoniedulogis.com
@harmoniedulogis

Libellule Brocante
26 Rue de Louviers
27490 La Croix-Saint-Leuffroy
Brocante objects
@libellule_brocante

La Longère
Showroom/studio: 27930 Irreville
(by appointment only)
Online store
Tableware
lalongeredecoration.fr
@la.longere.decoration

Stéphanie Mayeux
Showroom: Route de Randonnai,
61190 Irai (by appointment only)
Garden objects, furniture,
decorative objects
stephaniemayeux.com
@stephantiquedealer

Philippe Provot (see p. 164)
Brocante de Balines
Route Nationale 12
27130 Verneuil-sur-Avre
Antique furniture
@brocantedebalines

Arnaud de Saint-Martin (see p. 199)
Showroom: 17 Place de la République,
61130 Bellême
(by appointment only)
Doors and architectural antiques
@arnauddesaintmartin

Max Tetelin
199 Allée de la Plaine
76230 Isneauville
(by appointment only)
Brocante objects
@max.tetelin

Fanette Wallerand
93 Rue d'Amiens
76000 Rouen (by appointment only)
Paintings, antiques, and small items
@fanette.wallerand

Nouvelle Aquitaine

Les Puces de Charente
454 Rue des Merisiers
16430 Champniers
Brocante objects
@les_puces_de_charente

Occitanie

Atelier Vime
24 Quai du Rhône
30300 Vallabrègues
Wicker furniture
ateliervime.com • @ateliervime

Sylvie Bijoux
Marché à la Brocante,
Villeneuve-lès-Avignon
(see p. 229)

Cocagne de Sort
(Johanna Rodriguez)
Online store and stand at Marché
à la Brocante, Villeneuve-
lès-Avignon (see p. 229)
Antique jewelry, textiles, objects,
tableware
cocagnedesort.com
@cocagne_de_sort

Laure Vallez
Marché à la Brocante,
Villeneuve-lès-Avignon
(see p. 229)
Antique textiles
@laure.lingeancien

Village du Brocanteur
154 Avenue Ampère
30600 Vauvert
Brocante objects
levillagedubrocanteur.fr
@levillagedubrocanteur

Paris

AXS Design
12 Rue Saint-Sabin
75011 Paris
Brocante objects
axsdesign.fr
@axs_design

Au Bain Marie
56 Rue de l'Université
75007 Paris
Tableware
aubainmarie.com/en/
@aubainmarieparis

Belle Lurette
5 Rue du Marché Popincourt
75011 Paris
Mid-century furniture
@brocante_bellelurette

Benoit Joaillier
1 Rue de Bérite
75006 Paris
Antique jewelry
benoitjoaillier.com
@benoitjoallier

Blanche Patine
29 Rue des Vinaigriers
75010 Paris (by appointment only)
Terre de fer tableware
blanchepatine.com • @blanchepatine

Brunswick Art and Design
62 Rue de Turenne
75003 Paris
Mid-century furniture
brunswickad.com/en
@brunswick_art

Le Coin des Arts
89 Rue Legendre
75017 Paris
Antique furniture
@lecoindesarts

Courcelles Antiquités
97 Rue de Courcelles
75017 Paris
Antique furniture and paintings
courcelles-antiquites.com
@courcelles.antiquites

Epoque et Patines
Showroom: 75005 Paris
(by appointment only)
Stand at Foire de Chatou
(see p. 229)
Antique furniture and decorative items, *brocante* objects
epoquesetpatines.com
@epoqueetpatines

Galerie Deroyan
13 Rue Drouot
75009 Paris
Tapestries and rugs
deroyan.fr
@galeriederoyan

Galerie Jabert (Max Jabert, see p. 105)
Village Suisse, Grande Allée, nos. 90–91
78 Avenue de Suffren
75015 Paris
Antique tapestries and rugs
galeriejabert.com
@galerie_jabert

Galerie Paradis
7 Rue de Paradis
75010 Paris
Twentieth-century furniture
galerieparadis.fr/en
@galerieparadis.paris

Galerie Pénélope (Camille Cuvelier, see p. 140)
Showroom: 75018 Paris
(by appointment only)
Online store and stand at Foire de Chatou (see p. 229)
Jewelry
galeriepenelope.com
@galeriepenelope

Galerie Vauclair
(Laurence Vauclair, see p. 176)
24 Rue de Beaune
75007 Paris
Wicker furniture and majolica
galerie-vauclair.fr • @galerievauclaire

General Store Paris
35 Rue de Paradis
75010 Paris
Mid-century furniture
generalstoreparis.com
@generalstoreparis

L'Object Qui Parle
86 Rue des Martyrs
75018 Paris
Brocante objects and antique paintings
lobjetquiparle.fr
@lobjetquiparle

Stéphane Olivier
3 Rue de l'Université
75007 Paris
Furniture and decoration
stephaneolivier.fr
@galerie_stephane_olivier

Passion Tapis
Village Saint-Paul
15 Rue Saint-Paul
75004 Paris
Antique rugs
@passion_tapis_

Passy Brocante
5 Impasse des Carrières
75016 Paris
Tableware, furniture, and paintings
@passybrocante

Pierres de Julie
(Julie Mialet, see p. 147)
1 Avenue Paul Déroulède
75015 Paris
Antique and vintage jewelry
lespierresdejulie.com
@pierresdejulie

Clement Rosenzweig
Showroom: 75009 Paris
(by appointment only)
Stand at Foire de Chatou
Artwork and curiosities
@clementrosenzweig

Village Saint-Paul
Rue Saint-Paul
75004 Paris
Group of dealers; various specialties
@villagesaintpaulparis

Yveline Antiques
4 Rue de Furstemberg
75006 Paris
High-end antiques
yveline-antiquites.com/en/
@yvelineantiques

Paris Suburbs

Antiquités Rodriguez Décoration
15 Rue Jules Vallès
93400 Saint-Ouen-sur-Seine
Architectural antiques and large furniture
en.rodriguezantiquites.com
@antiquitesrodriguezdecoration

Brocante de La Bruyère
(Florence de Boissieu, see p. 204)
Showroom: 170 Avenue des Pépinières, Marché de Rungis, 94648 Rungis
(by appointment only)
Online store
Wholesale antiques, specialty tableware, and architectural antiques
brocantedelabruyere.com
@brocantedelabruyere

Sophie Cougoule-Devergne
Marché Serpette
93400 Saint-Ouen-sur-Seine
French and Italian chandeliers
@la_boutique_de_sophie

Galerie Laurent Cohen
7 Côte de la Guériauderie
78490 Grosrouvre
Yvelines
Antique paintings
@galerie_laurent_cohen

Lefebvre Antiquités (Sylvie Lefebvre)
Showroom: 58 Rue George Sand, 91120 Palaiseau
(by appointment only)
Stand at Foire de Chatou and at Salon des Antiquaires, Saint-Sulpice (see p. 229)
Antique jewelry
@franceantiquelefebvre

Lila K
Allée 1, Stands 7 and 8
Marché Paul Bert
93400 Saint-Ouen-sur-Seine
Wicker and tableware
@lila_k_antiques

Thibault Nossereau
Allée 3
Marché Paul Bert
93400 Saint-Ouen-sur-Seine
Antique furniture
@thibault_nossereau

Rue
St. SABIN
PALEMON - PORTE -

Un Singe en Hiver
87–88 Marché Dauphine
93400 Saint-Ouen-sur-Seine
High-end antiques
unsingenhiver.com

Les Tables d'Eva
(Eva Cwajg, see p. 88)
110 Rue des Rosiers
Marché Serpette
93400 Saint-Ouen-sur-Seine
Tableware
lestablesdeva.fr
@lestablesdeva

Provence

L'Art et La Manière
L'Île aux Brocantes
7 Avenue des Quatre Otages
84800 L'Isle-sur-la-Sorgue
Furniture and tableware
@lartetlamaniere_antiques

Atelier des Textiles Anciens
(Jérôme Prévost, see p. 126)
Showroom: 50 Rue Monge,
13150 Tarascon
(by appointment only)
Stand at Marché à la Brocante,
Villeneuve-lès-Avignon (see p. 229)
Eighteenth- and nineteenth-century
textiles
@atelier_textiles_anciens

Boutique de l'Antiquaire
9 Rue du Grand Pré
84160 Lourmarin
Furniture, dyed linens, and paintings
@laboutiquedel'antiquaire

Brocante and Co.
11 Avenue de l'Arrousaire
84000 Avignon
(by appointment only)
Brocante objects
@brocanteandco

Dickinson Antiquities (Kate Dickinson,
see p. 65)
Village des Antiquaires de la Gare
2 bis Avenue de l'Egalité
84800 L'Isle-sur-la-Sorgue
Antique silver
dickinsonantiquities.com
@k8silverplate

The Foraged Studio
(Mike Sajnoski, see p. 43)
Studio: Eygalières (by appointment
only)
Online store and stands at
Marché à la Brocante,
Villeneuve-lès-Avignon,
and Brocante d'Eygalières
(see p. 229)
Artwork, curiosities, and *brocante*
objects
mikesajnoski.com
@mike_sajnoski

La Galerie de Cotignac
37 Cours Gambetta
83570 Cotignac
Antique and vintage art
lagaleriecotignac.com
@lagaleriecotignac

Galerie Isabelle de Lafage
Hôtel Dongier
15 Esplanade Robert Vasse
84800 L'Isle-sur-la-Sorgue
Antique paintings
@isabelledelafage

Hôtel Dongier
15 Esplanade Robert Vasse
84800 L'Isle-sur-la-Sorgue
Group of dealers; various specialties
hoteldongierantiquites.fr
@hotel_dongier_antiquites

L'Île aux Brocantes
7 Avenue des Quatre Otages
84800 L'Isle-sur-la-Sorgue
Group of dealers; various specialties
@lile_aux_brocantes

Maison d'Inès
100 Rue Saint-Pierre
84400 Apt
Brocante objects
@lamaisondinesenprovence

Mémoires d'un Âne
Hôtel Dongier
15 Esplanade Robert Vasse
and
5 Avenue des Quatre Otages
84800 L'Isle-sur-la-Sorgue
Furniture
memoiresdunane.fr
@memoires_d_un_ane

Les Puces de Fifi
20 Boulevard Fifi-Turin
13010 Marseille
Group of dealers; various specialties
@lespucesdefifi

Frederic de la Rue
Hôtel Dongier
15 Esplanade Robert Vasse
84800 L'Isle-sur-la-Sorgue
Antique furniture and paintings
@frederic34delarue

Sylvie Bijoux
Foire Saint-Siffrein
Hôtel de Ville
Place Maurice Charretier
84200 Carpentras
Jewelry

Village des Antiquaires de la Gare
2 bis Avenue de l'Egalité
84800 L'Isle-sur-la-Sorgue
Group of dealers; various specialties
@villagedesantiquairesdelagare

Auction Houses

Aguttes
164 bis Avenue Charles-de-Gaulle
92200 Neuilly-sur-Seine
aguttes.com/en/
@aguttes_

Bonhams
6 Avenue Hoche
Paris 75008
bonhams.com • @bonhams1793

Christie's
9 Rue Matignon
75008 Paris
christies.com • @christiesinc

Digard
17 Rue Drouot
75009 Paris
digard.com/en/
@digard_auction

Drouot
9 Rue Drouot
75009 Paris
drouot.com/en • @drouot_paris

Millon
19 Rue de la Grange Batlière
75009 Paris
millon.com
@millon_auction

Sotheby's
83 Rue du Faubourg Saint-Honoré
75008 Paris
sothebys.com/en/
@sothebys

Fairs and Markets

Alsace

Marché Européen de la Brocante et du Design
Place Broglie
67000 Strasbourg
Six weekends in June–October, 8 a.m.–6 p.m.

Bordeaux

Brocante des Quinconces
Place des Quinconces
33000 Bordeaux
Two weeks in April and November, 10 a.m.–6 p.m.

Puces de Saint-Michel
17 Rue des Faures
33000 Bordeaux
Tuesday, Thursday, Friday, and Sunday, 6 a.m.–1 p.m.

Brittany

Braderie du Canal Saint-Martin
Canal Saint-Martin
35000 Rennes
Third Sunday in September, 8 a.m.–6 p.m.

Puces de Rennes
Mail François Mitterrand
35000 Rennes
Second Sunday of the month, 9 a.m.–6 p.m.

Salon des Antiquaires
Rue de la Vallée Verte
35300 Saint-Méloir-des-Ondes
Three days in mid-August, hours vary

Burgundy

Brocante de Beaune
Place Carnot
21200 Beaune
Saturday, 7 a.m.–1 p.m.

Puces de Belfort
Places d'Armes
90000 Belfort
First Sunday of the month, March–December, 7 a.m.–12:30 p.m.

Côte d'Azur

Brocante du Cours Saleya
Le Cours Saleya
06300 Nice
Monday, 7 a.m.–5 p.m.

Hauts-de-France

Puces de Compiègne
Town center
60200 Compiègne
Last weekend of June, 8 a.m.–7 p.m.

Réderie d'Amiens
Town center, 80000 Amiens
First Sunday of October, second Sunday of April, from 5 a.m.

Lille

Braderie de Lille
City center
59000 Lille
First weekend in September, last weekend in March, Saturday 8 a.m.–Sunday 6 p.m. (nonstop)

Loire

Brocante de Chambord
Château de Chambord
41250 Chambord
May 1, 7.30 a.m.–6 p.m.

Brocante de Tours
Boulevard Béranger
37000 Tours
Fourth Sunday of the month, 7 a.m.–7 p.m.

Puces de Montsoreau
Quai de la Loire
49730 Montsoreau
Second Sunday of the month, 9 a.m.–6 p.m.

Lyon

Puces du Canal
Rue Eugène Pottier
69100 Villeurbanne, Lyon
Thursday and Saturday, 7 a.m.–1 p.m.
Sunday, 7 a.m.–3 p.m.

Normandy

Brocante de Trouville
Place Maréchal de Tassigny
14360 Trouville-sur-Mer
Fourth Saturday of the month, 9 a.m.–6 p.m.

Foire des Andaines
Rue de l'Hippodrome
61140 Bagnoles-de-l'Orne
Second weekend in May, 5 a.m.–7 p.m.

Foire à la Brocante
Cour du Presbytère
27260 Morainville-Jouveaux
Long weekend in mid-August, 10 a.m.–6 p.m.

Grande Brocante de Lisieux
Town center
14100 Lisieux
Third weekend in November, 5 a.m.–6 p.m.

Puces Rouennaises
Parc des Expositions de Rouen
46 Avenue des Canadiens
76120 Grand Quevilly
Friday–Sunday in mid-January, 10 a.m.–8 p.m. (7 p.m. on Saturday, 6 p.m. on Sunday)

Village des Antiquaires
Barfleur Port
50760 Barfleur
Four days in late August, 10 a.m.–7 p.m.

Occitanie

Foire aux Antiquités et à la Brocante
Promenade des Marronniers
30700 Uzès
Mid-July, 8 a.m.–7 p.m.

Brocante des Allées
Allées Forain-François Verdier
31000 Toulouse
First weekend of the month, Friday–Sunday, 9.30 a.m.–6 p.m.

Foire de Barjac
Village center
30430 Barjac
Easter weekend and August 15, 9 a.m.–6 p.m.

Foire à la Brocante de Pézenas
17 Avenue de Verdun
34120 Pézanas
First Sunday in May, second Sunday in October, 8 a.m.–6 p.m.

Marché à la Brocante
Place Charles David
30400 Villeneuve-lès-Avignon
Saturday, 8 a.m.–1 p.m.

Marché de Saint-Aubin
Place Saint-Aubin / Boulevard Michelet
31000 Toulouse
Saturday, 7 a.m.–2 p.m.

Paris

Brocante du Marais
Place des Vosges
75003/75004 Paris
One weekend in mid-October, 7 a.m.–7 p.m.

Brocante de Passy
5 Impasse des Carrières
75016 Paris
Tuesday–Saturday, 11 a.m.–7 p.m.

Marché de Livres Anciens et d'Occasion
104 Rue Brancion
75015 Paris
Saturday and Sunday, 9 a.m.–6 p.m.

Puces d'Aligre
Place d'Aligre
75012 Paris
Tuesday and Sunday, 8 a.m.–2 p.m.
Saturday, 8 a.m.–3 p.m.

Puces de Vanves
Avenue Georges Lafenestre
75014 Paris
Saturday and Sunday, 7.30 a.m.–1 p.m.

Salon des Antiquaires
Place Saint-Sulpice
75006 Paris
Ten days in June and October, 11 a.m.–8 p.m.

Salon de la Bastille
Bassin de l'Arsenal and Place de la Bastille
75004/75012 Paris
Ten days in November, 11 a.m.–7 p.m.

Undesignable Market
32 Rue des Fossés Saint-Bernard
75005 Paris
One Sunday in March, June, and September, 6:30 a.m.–6 p.m.

Village Suisse
78 Avenue de Suffren
75015 Paris
Friday–Monday, 11 a.m.–7 p.m.

Paris Suburbs

Brocante du Grand Parquet
Stade Equestre du Grand Parquet
Route d'Orléans
77300 Fontainebleau
November 11 and July 14, 6 a.m.–6 p.m.

Foire de Chatou
Île des Impressionnistes
78400 Chatou
Ten days in March and September, 10 p.m.–7 p.m.

Puces de Saint-Ouen
Rue des Rosiers
93400 Saint-Ouen-sur-Seine
Friday, 8 a.m.–12 p.m.
Saturday–Monday, 10 a.m.–6 p.m.

Le Terrain
19 Quai Réné Richard
Fontaine-le-Port
77590 Seine-et-Marne
Fourth weekend of the month, check locally for opening times

Village des Antiquaires
13 Passage de la Geôle
78000 Versailles
Friday–Sunday, 11 a.m.–7 p.m.

Provence

Brocante de Carpentras
Parking des Platanes
Avenue Jean Jaurés
84200 Carpentras
Sunday, 9 a.m.–5 p.m.

Brocante d'Eygalières
Village center
13810 Eygalières
Last Sunday of the month, 8 a.m.–5 p.m.

Brocante Le Jas des Roberts
Chemin de Négresse
83310 Cagolin
Sunday, 8 a.m.–2 p.m.

Salon d'Antiquité
Le Grand Jardin
194 Rue Comtesse de Villeneuve
83440 Fayence
Nine days at the end of October and end of December, 10.a.m.–6 p.m.

Village des Antiquaires de la Gare
Town center
84000 L'Isle-sur-la-Sorgue
Friday–Sunday, 8 a.m.–2 p.m.

Useful Websites

brocabrac.fr
vide-greniers.org

PAGE 226
Faded indigo linen shirts still hold immense charm.

PAGE 227
At the Foire de Chatou, it's not unusual to find complete sets of antique china.

FACING PAGE
Taxidermy pieces are often available to purchase and add a whimsical touch to home décor.

Insider Tips for Antiquing

Antiquing is as much about the thrill of discovery as it is about the satisfaction of a well-made purchase. In France, dealers are generally friendly, knowledgeable, and open to discussion, and are often delighted to share insights about their wares.

However, they are, above all, observers of tradition, and a single misstep could earn you the dreaded *"c'est pas possible"* [it's not possible] from a displeased vendor. Knowing when to ask questions and how to negotiate politely, while respecting the dealer's expertise, will go a long way.

A few simple rules can help avoid any misunderstandings and ensure your dealings run smoothly. Here are some tips.

Smile ... a lot! Everyone prefers a smiling client.

Don't be shy about showing your interest in the history of an item. Vendors love discerning clients who are as appreciative of origins as design.

Take your time. You'll often find vendors or stores selling a lot of merchandise. Piles of objects can make it very easy to pass by without noticing what's really there. Don't hurry, inspect carefully, shop with a friend, and help each other to look out for that something special.

Keep your eyes and mind open. It's rarely a good idea to shop with a wish list in hand. By focusing too closely on crossing items off a list, you'll miss out on unexpected finds. Go with an open mind and be ready to be surprised.

Secure your finds. At fairs and markets, if you are thinking about purchasing a piece or negotiating the price, keep your hands on it. This is a sign to other potential buyers that you have first dibs. If you decide not to buy, then put the item down so it is free for someone else to snap up.

Be discreet. It is not the French custom to exclaim loudly or show too much excitement. Contain your joy and avoid drawing attention to yourself. An unobtrusive buyer gets better deals.

Don't flash your money around. In a rural *brocante* or at a small vendor's store especially, it looks out of place to pull a large roll of bills from your pocket when paying. Store your money in different pockets, or in a money belt to keep your hands free. If you buy something expensive and have to pay with a large quantity of cash, then deal with the vendor as discreetly as possible.

Agree on a fair price and keep your word. Don't push too hard when negotiating. Most vendors will have some flexibility, but don't expect them to drop their price too far. If you are unsure of a price, write the numbers down on a piece of paper to avoid any confusion. Once a price has been agreed, the purchase should take place immediately. It is considered rude to barter and obtain a discount, and then not buy.

Take risks. Dealers are more open to negotiating at opening or closing. If visiting a market or fair during peak hours—and you're feeling brave enough to risk losing the piece—return to the stand later in the day. You might get a better price if the item is still available.

Keep your hands free. When buying at a fair such as Chatou, it is quite usual to pay for goods but leave them with the vendor while you continue to shop. Well-organized fairs may even have a porter service, allowing your purchases to be collected in one fell swoop. Once you pay for your goods, make a note of where they are within the fair. If you are taking your items home in your own car, head to the commissary's booth when you're ready and request a pickup. If you have hired a shipper, give them the list of purchases, with the dealer's name, a description of the objects, and the location of the vendor at the fair; they will handle collection, wrapping as they go, and deliver to your chosen address.

Work with a shipper. If you plan to buy furniture or large quantities of antiques, contact shippers beforehand to get an idea of costs and details of the shipping process. For one-off purchases at the larger fairs, it is likely that shippers will be present and ready to help in person. At smaller fairs or antique stores, you can ask your shipper for a quote for collection, protection, and shipping. If you are buying in quantity and agree to work with a shipper, you will probably be given a buying book to note down the details of each item—it will be assigned a reference number and you will receive a label to attach to your purchases. The buying book is in triplicate pages: one for you, one for the vendor, and one for the shipper. Make sure you take pictures of everything you buy—it's surprising how easy it is to lose track.

Protect the goods. When buying fragile pieces, it's reasonable to expect the vendor to provide basic protection or wrapping. Goods are usually wrapped in newspaper, which suffices for short trips, but for longer journeys or for delicate items like glassware, bring your own boxes or bubble wrap. Some vendors may bag smaller items, but this isn't guaranteed—having reusable bags on hand makes shopping easier.

Useful Phrases

Buying an antique—be it a painting, chair, or dinner service—is first and foremost a conversation. Getting to know the vendor is as much a part of the process as the purchase itself, and can greatly influence both the price and your connection to the piece. Of course, dealers want to make a sale, but they also take an interest in where their prized possessions are going and who will enjoy them next.

A genuine effort to speak the language is always appreciated, so don't hesitate to begin in French and fall back on English when necessary. If the thought of speaking in French fills you with dread, simply smile, start with a friendly "*bonjour*," and ask the vendor if they speak English. And if they don't, you'll be surprised at how much can be understood through expressions and gestures!

Here are a few key phrases in French to get you started.

Negotiation

How much is it?	*C'est combien ?*
How much if I take them both/all three/all of them?	*C'est combien si je prends les deux/les trois/tout ?*
Would you take ten (euros)?	*Ça peut faire dix (euros) ?*
It's a good/bad deal.	*C'est une bonne/mauvaise affaire.*
Can I pay in cash?	*Je peux payer en liquide ?*
Can I pay by card?	*Je peux payer par carte ?*
Do you have any others/more?	*Vous en avez d'autres ?*
Beyond my budget, but thank you.	*Trop cher pour moi, merci.*
I'll offer you...	*Je vous propose...*
I'll think about it.	*Je vais réfléchir.*
Do you ship?	*Vous faites des envois ?*
Can I pick it up later?	*Je peux le récupérer plus tard ?*

Condition

Perfect	*Impeccable*
Good as new	*Comme neuf*
Never been used	*Jamais utilisé*
Damaged/very damaged	*Abimé/très abimé*
Split/cracked	*Fendu/fissuré/fêlé*
Showing signs of wear and tear	*Usé*
Pierced	*Troué*
Stamped	*Estampillé*
What size is the...?	*Quelles sont les dimensions de... ?*
How old is it?	*Ça date de quand ?*
Century	*Siècle* (e.g., *XVIII*e *siècle* = eighteenth century)
In its authentic, used condition (with patina and signs of wear and tear)	*Dans son jus*
What you see is what you get	*Dans l'état*
Discounted	*Soldé*
Renovated/restored	*Rénové/restauré*
Repaired	*Réparé*
Secondhand	*D'occasion* (sometimes shortened to *d'occas'*)

Selected Bibliography

Books

Bédoyère, Camilla de la. *Art Nouveau*. London: Flame Tree Illustrated, 2005.

Blunt, Wilfrid. *The Art of Botanical Illustration*. London: Collins, 1967.

Montaigne, Michel de. *Essays of Montaigne*. Selected and illustrated by Salvador Dalí. Translated by Charles Cotton. New York: Double Day & Company, 1947.

O'Mahoney, Mike. *World Art: The Essential Illustrated History*. London: Flame Tree Illustrated, 2006.

Riondet, Geoffray. *Antique French Jewelry: 1800–1950*. Paris: Éditions Flammarion, 2024.

Websites

(All websites accessed September 15, 2025)

1.75 Paris. "The Top Auction Houses in Paris." Blog, August 1, 2023. 175paris.com/en/blog/the-top-auction-houses-in-paris/

Antic Store. "Les styles." Le magazine des Arts décoratifs & des Beaux-Arts. anticstore.com/style/index.php

L'Antiquaire Parisien. "Définitions des termes du vocabulaire artistique et antiquaire." Blog de l'Antiquité parisienne: Les Antiquaires de Paris. antiquaireparisien.fr/vocabulaire-de-lantiquaire/

Antiques World. "Caring for Antique Furniture." antiquesworld.co.uk/caring-for-antique-furniture/

Basch, Sophie. "Les Demoiselles d'Avignon, de Schliemann à Picasso." Conference. Association Culturelle Egypto-Suisse, March 5, 2025. aces-geneve.ch/67090/les-demoiselles-davignon-de-schliemann-a-picasso/

Berganza. "Jewellery after the French Revolution." berganza.com/knowledge/jewellery-history/history/jewellery-after-the-french-revolution

Les Bijoux des Français. "The Jewels of the French." bijouxregionaux.fr/en/

Biodiversity Heritage Library. "The Botanical Art of Redouté." Blog, June 29, 2017. blog.biodiversitylibrary.org/2017/06/the-botanical-art-of-redoute.html

Christofle. "Care Guidance." Blog de Christofle. christfole.com/eu_en/care-advice

Decorative Collective. "How to Look After Antique Wooden Furniture." Blog. decorativecollective.com/blog/how-to-look-after-antique-wooden-furniture

Douane française. "Garantie des Métaux Précieux." October 2009. douane.gouv.fr/sites/default/files/uploads/files/2019-09/garantie-metaux-france.pdf

Drouot. "How to bid on Drout.com." Blog, May 16, 2025. drouot.com/en/hotel-drouot/actualite/102681-

Estarziau, Priscilla. "Restauration." La Galerie des Glaces. 2021. miroirsanciens.com/restauration

Heritage de France. "Comment faire expertiser un bijou ancien." heritage-de-france.fr/expertise-rachat/expertise-de-bijoux-anciens-et-recents

Jack Weir & Sons. "Tout ce que vous devez savoir sur les bijoux français." Blog, May 27, 2022. jackweirandsons.com/fr/blogs/news/all-you-need-to-know-about-french-jewelry

La Louème. "How to Properly Care for Your Vintage Tableware and Glassware." laloueme.com/blogs/news/vintage-wash-and-care-instructions

Madame de la Maison. "How to Clean and Care for Antiques: Dinnerware and Glassware." Blog, November 9, 2012. madamedelamaison.com/blogs/putting-it-all-on-the-table/how-to-clean-and-care-for-antiques-dinnerware-and-glassware

Maison Fête et Cie. "Caring for Antiques." maisonfeteetcie.com/pages/caring-for-antiques

Maison Riondet. "Styles & Époques." Blog. maison-riondet.fr/blog/histoire-bijoux-anciens/bijoux-epoques/

Matt Camron Rugs and Tapestries. "Rug Guides: Antique Rugs." mattcamron.com/rug-guides/antique-rugs
Mercier Art. "Comment reconnaître un lustre ancien ?" mercier-art.com/guide-encheres/comment-reconnaitre-un-lustre-ancien/
Millon. "Estimation d'une tapisserie : prix et avis gratuits de nos experts." Actualités. millon.com/actualites/estimation-dune-tapisserie-prix-et-avis-gratuits-de-nos-experts
Millon. "Reconnaître un tapis ou une tapisserie Gobelins." Actualités. millon.com/actualites/reconnaitre-un-tapis-ou-une-tapisserie-gobelins
Montenon, Agathe. "The great French jewelry houses." Blog. agathemontenon.com/en/blogs/news/les-grandes-maisons-de-joaillerie-francaise
Nazmiyal Collection. "Collector's Corner: A Guide to Building a Valuable and Authentic Rug Collection." Blog, April 15, 2025. nazmiyalantiquerugs.com/blog/collectors-corner-a-guide-to-building-a-valuable-and-authentic-rug-collection/
Poulbenn. "Jargon d'un Métier." Blog, 2023. poulbenn.com/glossaire-jargon-metier
Shapero Rare Books. "Rare Book Collecting: A Beginner's Guide." Blog. shapero.com/blogs/bookshop-blog/rare-book-collecting-a-beginners-guide
Versailles Tourism. "Antiquarian district." en.versailles-tourisme.com/antiquarian-district.html
World of Books. "Old & Rare Book Care." worldofbooks.com/en-gb/pages/old-rare-book-care

Acknowledgments

As I delved into my memories of antique hunting over the past thirty years to research and write this book, I realized just how much I've learned from the hundreds of dealers, experts, and enthusiasts I've had the privilege to meet. I am eternally grateful for all the knowledge and tips that have been shared with me along the way. In particular, I wish to thank:

My family, for their never-ending encouragement in all that I get up to at My French Country Home, and for their patience through the years each time I've driven home from an antique fair with the most unlikely purchases in the trunk.

My dear friend Laurent Escoulin, who taught me so much about the process of buying antiques, and who shared his expertise with great generosity.

The many antique dealers all around France who opened their doors for our photos, and patiently answered my many questions. A special *merci* to the organizers of the Foire de Chatou, for the privileged access we have to their events.

Madeleine Piggott, who meticulously seconded me in the writing of this book, rereading and improving on texts, doing all-important research, and keeping us on track to hit deadlines.

The team at My French Country Home for their unfailing enthusiasm for the project.

Kate Mascaro and Helen Adedotun at Flammarion, whose professional expertise and attention to detail allowed this book to take shape. Thank you for your guidance and for inviting me to write this book.

Joanna Maclennan and Franck Schmitt for their photography, and their willingness to go the extra mile in the quest for the right shot.

And, finally, the many people who have joined me over the years to go antique and *brocante* shopping. Thank you for your enthusiasm and trust. It's been a joy to share with you my love of all things French.

Index

Page numbers in *italics* refer to illustrations

PAGES 236–240
Books can lend essential touches of color. A collection of embroidered or painted handheld fans from the eighteenth century. English and French flatware with mother-of-pearl handles. Bundles of seventeenth-century manuscripts tied with a simple string bow. Fragments of carved stone and plaster castings.

TACITE
BROTIER,
BITAUBÉ.
OEUVRES
D'HOMÈRE.
TOME II.
1828.
Cazotte

WEMBLEY
1924